White-Collar Crime:
A 20th-Century Crisis

White-Collar Crime: A 20th-Century Crisis

August Bequai

Lexington Books
D.C. Heath and Company
Lexington, Massachusetts
Toronto

Library of Congress Cataloging in Publication Data

Bequai, August.
    White-collar crime: a 20th-century crisis

    Bibliography: p.
    Includes index.
    1. White collar crimes—United States. I. Title.
HV6791.B46   364.1'63'0973   77-11242
ISBN 0-669-01900-3

Published simultaneously in Canada.

Printed in the United States of America.

International Standard Book Number: 0-669-01900-3

Library of Congress Catalog Card Number: 77-11242

For My Mother and Father

Contents

Preface

Recently, four businessmen were convicted in what has been called a "massive robbery" of more than 40,000 investors in more than 30 states. The defendants had sold them approximately 70,000 real estate lots, some for as much as $10,000 each. Investors were promised that these lots were developed, and that planned communities would be established on them. Before the fraud was finally uncovered, the investors had lost more than $150 million.

In Chicago, a federal grand jury charged that a large chemical firm had falsified the laboratory tests of its best selling pesticides; the actual tests had revealed that these chemicals might be cancer causing. In a national investigation that spans several port cities, investigators are looking into allegations that import agents and companies may have been involved in a multimillion dollar scheme of payoffs and kickbacks; government sources indicate that the questionable payments may run as high as $100 million.

These cases serve to illustrate a growing problem—the predatory practices of white-collar criminals. This class of felon is not the child of poverty; he preys on poor and rich alike; corporations and consumers alike fall his victims. He is as old as ancient Egypt; yet modern technology has given him awesome powers. At the flick of a switch, he can instruct computers to transfer millions of dollars; electronically, he can create false assets and earnings. Modern telecommunications place him in contact with associates all over the world. In Nigeria, he sacks the state's treasury of more than $17 million; in England, he is involved in foreign currency frauds; in Argentina, he sets up corporate shells to funnel funds to revolutionary groups. With the growing technology and interdependence among nations, he represents a glimpse of what may await us.

Acknowledgments

In writing this book I would like to thank my many friends and associates for their assistance and support. Principally, I would like to express my appreciation to my research assistants, Joe Kalet and Teuta Bequai. I would also like to thank Philip Manuel, Fred Asselin, Waverly A. Yates, David Saari, John V. Graziano, John A. Jenkins, Lewis Schneider, Dennis Goldman, and my typist, Linda Thomas.

When I first began work on this book, I knew that it would be no easy endeavor. The book, hopefully, will be only a beginning in this arena; there is room for much more work. The area is an important one, and hopefully both scholars and jurists will devote attention to it. Those who purport to have easy solutions delude both themselves and others.

Introduction

As part of their class work, I recently assigned my students reports on various areas of white-collar crime. One of the students gave a report on frauds in the antipoverty programs: "The $30 Billion War—That We Lost." She noted that Congressional investigators had uncovered massive frauds in these programs and the agencies that were established to administer them. For example, one large agency, with an annual budget of over $500 million, was said to have spent millions of dollars on questionable projects. In one year alone, $30 million had been spent on "policy research," but Congressional investigators were unable to determine exactly what the agency had done with this money. Other antipoverty agencies were found to be spending federal funds for the personal entertainment of their employees; the director of one antipoverty agency had hired, as a consultant, an individual who had previously been convicted for misappropriating federal antipoverty funds.

Other students also gave their reports; one student commented on kickbacks in the construction industry; he cited the case of a Mr. X who had paid more than $100,000 in kickbacks and received a $500 fine. Another student reported on a U.S. Senate probe into medicare frauds; investigators had found that doctors were stealing more than $300 million annually by padding and falsifying their claims. One student reported on sentencing in white-collar crime cases. He noted that one case he had studied involved 15 executives from large paperboard box firms; they had been convicted of criminal price fixing. The judge sentenced some of these to prison terms ranging from 5 to 45 days; that same judge, several days before, had sentenced a young defendant to several years in prison for auto theft.

This book is an outgrowth of the many questions that both my students and clients often ask me: "What is white-collar crime?" "What can be done to halt it?" "What is law enforcement doing about it?" and many other similar questions. Hopefully, in this book, I have addressed myself to some of these questions; many more remain to be answered in other books.

Chapter 1 seeks to define the problem of white-collar crime, while Chapters 2 and 3 attempt to explain why both jurists and academics have long neglected its study and classification. Chapter 4 deals with frauds in the securities industry; the next four chapters address themselves to various other categories of frauds, for example, in the area of bankruptcy, bribes to both corporate and public officials, consumer frauds, and frauds in government contracts and programs.

Chapters 9 and 10 deal with insurance swindles and insider-related frauds, such as embezzlement and pilferage by employees. The next four chapters deal with monopolies and price fixing (antitrust), computer-related crimes, offenses against our physical environment, and tax frauds. Chapter 15 deals with the influx of organized crime into the white-collar crime area and the need to adopt a new strategy, and policy, in combating it. Chapters 16 and 17 deal with problems investigators and prosecutors face in white-collar crime cases and the need to modernize these two key law enforcement mechanisms. Chapter 18 deals with problems related to litigating white-collar crime cases, such as hearsay and best-evidence-rule roadblocks. Finally, Chapter 19 deals with crimes of the future, those made possible by our growing automation and technology; the failure of our present laws to adequately deal with them.

White-collar crime is on the increase; the cost to society is also increasing, not only in terms of money and property stolen yearly by these felons, but also in terms of the loss of confidence and respect by the public at large in our institutions of government. With the growth in federal spending in both defense and social programs, white-collar crime has found fertile ground. It is a "growth industry." Unless we study it and develop tools to deal with it effectively, we may be witnessing only the tip of the iceberg.

1 Defining the Problem

The former financial officer of one of the nation's largest tire manufacturers was recently indicted on charges that he stole more than $500,000 from his former employer.[1] To add further drama to the case, prosecutors alleged that the money came from a secret corporate slush fund used to make illegal political contributions. In another instance, the chairman of one of the nation's largest sewage hauling firms and four other individuals were charged with being involved in a scheme that may have paid more than $1 million in bribes to local political figures in the midwest.[2]

The preceding cases serve to illustrate a serious and growing problem in both this country and abroad—white-collar crime. Experts note that the annual cost of this form of crime, domestically, exceeds $40 billion.[3] White-collar crime covers every facet of our economy and society; neither rich nor poor is able to escape its clutches. It does not discriminate among its victims. Those who are responsible for this type of crime come from all strata of society; no profession is excluded. For example, two former judges, one of them a federal judge, were said to have been silent partners in a company that had an exclusive concession contract with one of the nation's largest airports.[4] The intimate involvement of such responsible members of the judiciary in such secret agreements presents a clear picture of the breadth and depth of white-collar crime in America.

What is White-Collar Crime?

Early criminologists viewed crime in terms of deviant behavior, which was itself considered to be an outgrowth of poverty.[5] According to this view (which prevailed in the eighteenth and nineteenth centuries), the social and physical conditions of the poor gave rise to antisocial behavior. However, Marxist scholars of the nineteenth and twentieth centuries viewed crime as an outgrowth of the class conflict. These two positions, the traditional and Marxist, still influence much of the studies in criminology.

In the 1930s, the traditional approach to crime came under attack as a result of earlier developments in this area. During the latter part of the nineteenth century, a series of laws had been enacted that outlawed much of the behavior associated with the robber barons of the post-Civil War era. Further, new policing agencies had been established (for example, the Interstate

Commerce Commission and the Federal Trade Commission) to police and control abuses in the business world. The scope of illegality had even been expanded to include offenses by the wealthy. It was in this environment that Edwin H. Sutherland began to attack traditional concepts and theories of crime.[6]

Sutherland noted that the explanations for crime could not be found in poverty alone, that criminality was a much more complex phenomena. For example, he noted that poverty is no explanation for the crimes of the rich and the professional segments of society. Studies were needed to explain these. Business-related crimes, as Sutherland called them, found expression most often in such behavior as the manipulation of stocks, price fixing, both commercial and political bribery, and false and misleading advertising.[7]

He reduced business crimes into two major categories: (1) those involving misrepresentation of corporate assets (such as stock manipulations, bankruptcy frauds, etc.) and (2) those involving the manipulation of power (such as political bribery).[8] Sutherland also noted that these criminals of the "suites" had been segregated from traditional criminals, and that their crimes were adjudicated by regulatory agencies, such as the Federal Trade Commission, thus shielding them from the traditional criminal justice apparatus. Their offenses were handled administratively, resulting only in minor fines; few offenders ever went to prison.

Sutherland's definition of white-collar crime was based largely on his observations and the horrors of the economic depression of the 1930s. For example, Sutherland points to numerous cases, involving large sums of money, where the felons went unpunished. One such individual, involved in a massive stock fraud, took his victims for more than $500 million and never saw the inside of a prison. Thus, it was only logical for Sutherland to conclude that these crimes were committed by individuals of high social status in the course of their occupations. In his time, and in his environment, only the wealthier classes had access to the requisite machinery to enact these multimillion dollar swindles.

The rising electronic revolution, simultaneous with the growth and sophistication of organized crime, had not surfaced yet in the 1930s and 1940s. The computer had not come into its own, nor had the criminal warlords of the cities attained the level of sophistication necessary to penetrate the legitimate business sector. Bankruptcy frauds, securities swindles, and union pension frauds were to surface later. Nevertheless, Sutherland was correct in stressing the role of the upper class in these crimes. Technology and mass communications would ultimately open those areas of criminal endeavor to all strata of society, but this change had not yet occurred.

White-collar crimes, like traditional crimes, are acts that are proscribed by law. There are numerous statutes at the federal and state levels that provide for fines or imprisonment or both for those individuals who violate them. Many of these laws deal with such areas as price fixing, securities frauds, environmental crimes, and so on (to be covered in later chapters). Like traditional crimes, white-collar offenses are viewed as a threat to the well-being of society. White-collar crimes, however, differ in two key respects from traditional offenses: (1) impact and (2) modus operandi. In terms of injury, white-collar crimes affect more individuals; in terms of money or lost property, these crimes are costlier than traditional offenses. In terms of modus operandi, white-collar criminals rely on deceit and concealment; they play on the naiveté of their victims and the near-universal greed of the individual. Force and physical violence play a secondary role.

Many times the victims of white-collar crime are not even aware of their plight. For example, the typical consumer may never know that the automobile he has purchased is in fact a "lemon." In addition to frequent reliance on the victim's ignorance, these crimes are also international in scope. A securities fraud may affect victims on several continents; price fixing may affect the peasant in India, just as it affects the farmer in this country. The multinational nature of business has made these crimes international.

The objective of these crimes, however, differs little from that of traditional offenses. The perpetrator seeks some gain in terms of either money or property or both; this may take the form of gaining some advantage over one's competitors, or obtaining services for free or at a reduced cost. At times, the felon may also seek to avoid an obligation, for example, to evade income tax laws or payment for services. The actor himself may have an upper-class background; he may be a professional or a clerk with access to a computer. The forum and the setting may differ from traditional crime; the objectives, however, are exactly the same—to gain at the expense of someone else. New technology has provided this group of felons with new capabilities, which make these criminals even more threatening.

Scope of the Problem

White-collar offenses can be perpetrated by individuals, partnerships, or corporations. Victims range from the average, unsuspecting consumer to the sophisticated banker; both young and old are open to attack. No individual or institution is immune to white-collar criminals. For example, one such group defrauded the Vatican out of millions of dollars in a sophisticated stock swindle; another group of white-collar felons defrauded several hundred children in a charity swindle. More than 50 banks in the last dozen years have gone into bankruptcy, in large part because of white-collar frauds; the prices of fuel, food, and housing have risen substantially because of similar price-fixing schemes.

White-collar crimes take on numerous forms; consumer frauds alone have been identified in more than 800 forms.[9] Bankruptcy frauds, tax swindles, and securities violations exclusively account for losses in the billions of dollars per year. Bribery and kickback schemes in the government contracts area increased the tax burden in one city alone by as much as 40 percent.[10] A single, massive computer fraud caused over $1 billion in losses to investors, and experts predict that more such crimes are in sight.

White-collar crime poses a threat not only in terms of its impact on the thousands of victims that are defrauded of their hard earned money, but also in terms of what the average citizen thinks of our system of justice. In a democracy, where consensus is the key stabilizing element, a cynical citizenry may signal the decay of that system. White-collar felons largely escape punishment because of the antiquated legal apparatus that is brought to bear against them. That apparatus is too cumbersome, ill-prepared, and easily manipulated to be an effective tool against white-collar crime. Consequently, a dual system of justice has come into being—one for the masses, who commit traditional offenses, and the other for a small select group of white-collar felons. The average citizen who witnesses white-collar felons escaping punishment understandably becomes cynical. When the majority of the citizenry comes to view our system of laws in this light, then democracy itself could be threatened. A segregated system of justice is no less divisive and damaging than a society segregated on the basis of race.

Notes

1. "Firestone Tire Ex-Finance Chief Indicted for $1 Million Theft from Payoff Fund," *Wall Street Journal*, October 26, 1977, p. 8.

2. Robert Warden, "Five Convicted in Chicago Sewage Contract Bribe Scheme," *Washington Post*, November 9, 1977, p. A-19.

3. Chamber of Commerce of the United States, *White Collar Crime* (Washington, D.C.: Chamber of Commerce of the United States, 1974), p. 6.

4. "Dailey Cohorts Accused," *Washington Post*, November 3, 1977, p. A-7.

5. James Q. Wilson, *Thinking About Crime* (New York/ Basic Books, 1975), p. 43.

6. Edwin H. Sutherland, "White Collar Criminality," in *White Collar Crime*, Gilbert Geis and Robert F. Neier, eds. (New York: Free Press, 1977), p. 38.

7. Ibid., p. 40.

8. Ibid.

9. Chamber of Commerce of the United States, *White Collar Crime*, p. 26.

10. Ibid., p. 5.

Why White-Collar Crime Has Been Neglected

In 1931 *The New York Times* reported several cases of fraud, each costing the public more than $1 million.[1] In a separate case, between 1929 and 1935, thousands of investors were fleeced of more than $500 million in an investment trust fund fraud.[2] In 1938 the Federal Bureau of Investigation's (FBI) most wanted public enemies stole less than $200,000; while during this same period, one white-collar felon stole $250 million.[3] One federal prosecutor, commenting on the problem of white-collar crime, wrote:

The popular view is that large numbers of white-collar criminals are victimizing the American citizenry. . . . As much as one would like to dismiss this view as folk myth, it is, in fact, embarrassingly accurate.[4]

White-collar crime is a growing problem that poses serious consequences for both law enforcement and the public alike. A recent U.S. Commerce Department study noted that businesses alone lose more than $30 billion annually to white-collar felons; this represents an 11 percent increase from the previous year.[5] White-collar crime, unfortunately, is not limited to the business world; consumers are also victimized. It also reaches individuals within the public sector; for example, a businessman recently pleaded guilty to lying to a grand jury that was investigating corruption in the federal government.[6]

There can be little doubt that white-collar crime will continue to rob society as it has in the past,[7] that modern technology has aggravated an already serious situation. White-collar crime victimizes millions of individuals; it robs businesses of billions of dollars annually; and it undermines the very legitimacy of our institutions. Despite all these factors, the criminal justice system still devotes little or no attention to this area. There are a number of reasons why so little research has been devoted to white-collar crime. Basically, there are four key factors: (1) the historical development of crime, (2) the approach to crime by traditional criminologists, (3) the infusion of ideology in the study of crime, and (4) the difficulty researchers face in attempting to study this particular area of criminal activity.

Historical Development of Crime

In tribal societies, crime is a strictly personal matter. An offense against the individual, his family, or relations becomes a personal affair between the offender and the offended. Either the individual or his relations take vengeance for the wrong done their bloodline. In modern societies, the matter is for the state to handle. Criminals are prosecuted and punished in the name of the state. This, however, was not always the case.

Our system of jurisprudence is an outgrowth of the historical evolution of England's system of laws. Our overall criminological approach to what we have come to consider deviant behavior is an outgrowth of European thought and philosophy (with primary influence from the English). With the fall of Rome, Europe entered what was later called the Dark Ages. A system of feudalism evolved, and the state came to be viewed as the personal manor of the ruling family (the monarch). Numerous dynasties emerged and declined, for example, the Carolingians, Normans, Plantagenets, Burgundians, Hapsburgs, Bourbons, and Hohenzollerns, to name a few. These families, at one time or another, ruled and controlled Europe.[8]

Although each dynasty had its own peculiar views and ideologies, they all had one thing in common: the state was their domain; treason to the state was treason against them. As Louis XIV would note, "I am the state." Because of this attitude, the monarchs and their underlings saw themselves as being above the law. Since the state was theirs to use as they pleased, they saw nothing wrong with their actions. It was not until the English revolted against King Charles I in the seventeenth century that the monarch was made subservient to the law.[9]

However, the English experience was an exception to the norm. Many of Europe's ruling families conducted themselves as "owners" of their states. The Hohenzollerns viewed themselves as the landlords of Germany; and for all practical purposes, they were. Thus, well after World War I, the upper classes in many countries in Europe and throughout the world viewed themselves as being above the law. Thus the modern law enforcement apparatus that began to take shape in the nineteenth century addressed itself to the poorer, more visible criminal element. The upper classes viewed themselves as being above the laws of the state; in many instances, their control of the prosecutorial and judicial machinery ensured them de facto immunity from prosecution. The evolving police forces concentrated their thrust in the area of traditional offenses committed by the lower classes.

Traditional Criminology

The explanation of why the upper classes enjoyed, for so long, de facto, if not legal, immunity from prosecution can be found not only in history, but also in the writings of jurists and criminologists. Starting with Cesare Beccaria (1738-1793), the father of modern criminology, the thrust of these scholars was reform oriented.[10] They were concerned with the plight of the weak and poor; the law, Beccaria wrote, should be applied equally to all classes in society. He had no suggestions as to how the upper classes should also be brought within the realm of the law. For example, who was to investigate and prosecute them? Beccaria himself made no note of the commercial frauds that plagued eighteenth century Europe, of the price fixing of food and necessities, or of the fact that these felons escaped punishment, unless they angered the monarch.

Edward Livingston (1734-1836), an American scholar, was a disciple of Beccaria.[11] He saw crime as an outgrowth of idleness, unemployment, and, like Beccaria, poverty. Criminal behavior, he noted, was learned through maturation and nurtured by a defective family background; it was the product of one's environment and subsequent associations. He further noted that laws had been made oppressive and unjust by the upper classes, but his thrust was directed toward assisting the criminal in finding a new life. For this he suggested religious instruction.

John Haviland (1792-1852), also an American, played a key role in laying the foundations of modern criminology.[12] He was largely influenced by Quaker dogma, and developed a penal model to reform the criminal. The latter was to be taught a trade, given religious instruction, and kept isolated from other felons. Once again, the thrust of his model was aimed at the lower classes. They needed instruction in how to be productive and law abiding, or so the thinking went.

Other scholars, both in this country and in Europe, also addressed the problem of crime. Karl Roeder (1806-1879) suggested that the criminal is like a child and must be put on the moral path once again.[13] Isaac Ray (1807-1881) explored science for an answer to crime; he wrote that crime could, in some cases, be an outgrowth of some mental defect.[14] Henry Maudsley (1835-1918) saw it as a degeneracy and blamed it on the individual's upbringing.[15] Cesare Lombroso (1835-1909) spoke of heredity and biological factors as being responsible for criminal behavior.[16]

Students of crime, from the eighteenth century onward have concentrated their studies and efforts on the lower classes. There are explanations for this. The industrial revolution, which gave rise to modern industry, finance, and banking, was little understood during much of this time. In addition, many of these writers were heavily influenced by the rise in new ideologies and political schools of thought. Socialism, anarchism, liberal democracy, communism, nihilism, and utopianism, to name a few, had emerged on the theater of Western civilization. The crimes of the upper classes were viewed in terms of politics rather than law. They were the acts of an immoral ruling elite rather than the illegal acts of a strata of society. In many instances, these ideologues were justified, for in nineteenth century Europe, the upper classes deemed themselves as being above the law. Well into the twentieth century, crimes by the professional and affluent sectors of society were viewed through a political prism. Those who attacked such acts did so along political lines; they, in turn, were labeled Communists and Socialists. The rising ideologies of the eighteenth and nineteenth centuries muddled the waters of criminology.

The Infusion of Ideology—the Marxist Approach

The mid-nineteenth century saw the rise of revolutions and political assassinations. It also witnessed the rise of Marxism and its ensuing impact on global history. Karl Marx (1818-1883), in his *Communist Manifesto*, further fused the study of criminology with political ideology.[17] In 1883 a group of European intellectuals founded the first Marxist party. This new ideology further politicized the study of criminology by injecting the view that the criminal in a bourgeoise society was prosecuted for his political opposition to the state; further, it portrayed the law as a tool of the ruling class, employed to oppress the lower classes.[18]

Marx saw his society as being engaged in a struggle between the ruling groups and the lower classes. The state, itself, was a tool of the former; law, and the entire legal apparatus, was their creature, to serve them and oppress the weak and poor. The ruling class perpetuated its rule through force and fraud. The answer, according to Marx, was the "revolution." This would give rise to a dictatorship of the proletariat, which in turn would lead the masses to true communism. Obviously, this quasi-religious approach to crime injected ideology into criminology. Thus, according to this view, the white-collar felon is acting out the frauds of his class; the answer is not to imprison or study him, but rather to destroy both him and his social group. It appears that those who attempted a serious study of white-collar crime were hampered, in part, by their utopian counterparts, and also by the more conservative elements of society, who saw them as Communists in disguise. This dual phobia impeded a serious study of white-collar crime well into the twentieth century.

The ideological turmoil of the last two centuries and the association, in the minds of many scholars, of crime with poverty led to a sidestepping of any serious study of white-collar crime. Further, it should also be noted that price fixing, security frauds, and consumer-related frauds were not outlawed, at least in this country, until the twentieth century. Other white-collar offenses, such as computer crimes and privacy-related crimes, only became matters of serious concern in the last dozen or more years.[19] Thus the law enforcement apparatus that grew and developed both in this country and in Europe neglected to deal with these nontraditional crimes because scholars of crime failed to address this area. They were heavily influenced by the history of their societies and by the raging ideological debates that engulfed their world. Some of these debates continue to hamper the study of white-collar crime today.

The Problem with Obtaining Data

Scholars and jurists must not bear the blame exclusively; data on white-collar crimes are difficult to obtain. The law enforcement apparatus in this country (more than 2000 federal agencies, commissions, and departments) is equally guilty of creating this problem. For example, although it is an easy matter to go to any court in this country and witness a trial or review documents relating to specific cases, the situation is somewhat different in the area of white-collar crime. Many of the federal agencies that conduct white-collar crime investigations (for example, the Federal Trade Commission, the Securities and Exchange Commission, the Department of Housing and Urban Development) do so in secrecy. Their files are not open to the public; if there is a disposition, the adjudication is usually handled internally in the form of an administrative hearing. In addition, many of these hearings are closed to the public.

Further, many of the agencies charged with the investigation and prosecution of these nontraditional crimes do not make their findings public. The data made available to the public are usually "doctored" to meet the political needs of the bureaucracy. Presently, it is difficult to obtain information on investigations that never surface in prosecution; for example, we are not told why an investigation was dropped, what the nature of the investigation was, who the parties involved were, and so on. Even when investigations do culminate in prosecution, the data that surface are usually watered down versions of the events as they actually occurred. Students of white-collar crime who collect data find that the agencies have done everything possible to keep the public, and academia, in the dark about their inner workings and investigations. This cloak of secrecy, we are told by the government agencies, is necessary in order for them to function as effective law enforcement instruments.

Scholars of white-collar crime therefore must break the chains of traditional scholasticism and smash the ideological prism employed in the past to interpret criminal behavior. They must also contend with the attempts of federal, and even local, agencies to conceal their workings from the public. Presently, at the federal level, statutes like the Freedom of Information Act (FOIA) have been employed with some success to open the bureaucracy; some of the states have also enacted similar legislation. Students of white-collar crime, unlike their predecessors, enjoy an environment free of the ideological conflicts of the turn of this century. Further, the quantity and quality of the data presently available to them exceeds that which

Sutherland had at his disposal. Scholars and jurists alike can no longer sweep this subject matter under the rug.

Notes

1. Edwin H. Sutherland, "White Collar Criminality," in *White Collar Crime*, Gilbert Geis and Robert F. Meier, eds. (New York: Free Press, 1977), p. 42.
2. Ibid., pp. 42, 43.
3. Ibid., p. 42.
4. Robert W. Ogren, "The Ineffectiveness of the Criminal Sanctions in Fraud and Corruption Cases: Losing the Battle Against White Collar Crime," *The American Criminal Law Review* XI (1973): 959.
5. Larry Kramer, "Thieves, Swindles Plague U.S. Business," *Washington Post*, November 18, 1977, p. F-1.
6. "Perjurer Gets Probation, Fine in HUD Probe," *Washington Post*, November 18, 1977, p. B-7.
7. U.S. Department of Commerce, *Crime in Service Industries* (Washington, D.C.: Government Printing Office, 1977), pp. 3-9.
8. See Hans Kohn, *Prelude to Nation-States* (Princeton, N.J.: Van Nostrand, 1967), pp. 1-13.
9. Cicely V. Wedgwood, "Revolutionary Tactics—and Charles I's Decisive Blunder," in *The Origins of the English Civil War*, Philip A.M. Taylor, ed. (Lexington, Mass.: D.C. Heath and Company, 1960), pp. 91-98.
10. Elio Monachesi, "Cesare Beccaria," in *Pioneers in Criminology*, Hermann Mannheim, ed. (Montclair, N.J.: Patterson Smith, 1972), pp. 36-51.
11. Joseph Mouledoux, "Edward Livingston," ibid., pp. 69-84.
12. Norman B. Johnson, "John Haviland," ibid., p. 107.
13. Klas Lithner, "Karl Roeder," ibid., p. 158.
14. Winfred Overholster, "Isaac Ray," ibid., p. 177.
15. Peter Scott, "Henry Maudsley," ibid., p. 208.
16. Marvin E. Wolfgang, "Cesare Lombroso," ibid., p. 232.
17. Gwendolen M. Carter, *The Government of the Soviet Union* (New York: Harcourt, Brace & World, 1967), pp. 28-41.
18. William J. Chambliss, "Functional and Conflict Theories of Crime," in *Whose Law What Order*, William J. Chambliss and Milton Mankoff, eds., (New York: Wiley, 1976), pp. 7-9.
19. Computer crime began to attract national attention only in the early 1970s. See August Bequai, *Computer Crime* (Lexington, Mass.: Lexington Books, D.C. Heath, 1977), for further details on computer crime.

3

Identifying White-Collar Crimes

In the spring of 1950, several masked men robbed the Brink's corporation of more than $2 million.[1] The crime was reported by newspapers in the United States and abroad; movies were made, and numerous books written. Several days before the statute of limitations was to expire, the robbers were apprehended; half of them received life sentences. In the summer of 1963, an English train was robbed of more than $7 million.[2] The train had been carrying more than a ton of bank notes. Within several months, the gang was discovered and prosecuted. Hollywood movies and numerous books followed. The robbers became part of popular myth; their names were known by all. The setting and the participants were both familiar to the public. They filled the image of what crime and criminals represent to the common man.

In the 1930s, the citizens of a large Midwestern city lost more than $50 million to a fraud involving dishonest businessmen and city officials.[3] However, no movies were ever made based on this crime; the names of those responsible have long since been forgotten; the victims never saw their money again. In a similar case, the mayor of a large Eastern city bilked contractors out of more than $1 million in kickbacks.[4] A businessman in a Southern state was charged with defrauding several firms out of more than $20 million, and of bribing federal officials.[5] No Hollywood movies were ever produced as a result of these crimes; the names of those involved have been forgotten. The stage and the actors were both somewhat different. These were not men and women driven by poverty and oppressive conditions; they were white-collar felons, as yet little understood or studied.

The Actors in White-Collar Crime

Consumer fraud is said to account for more than $20 billion in losses annually to the public;[6] commercial and political bribery may run as high as $10 billion;[7] even the more conservative estimates place the cost of white-collar crime in excess of $30 billion.[8] Yet who are these actors? Who are the victims? What motivates such felons? A personal acquaintance of the author, who had spent more than a dozen years studying traditional felons, provided a terse answer to these questions: "I don't know." A prison psychiatrist was asked if any studies had been conducted involving white-collar felons; he knew of none. The stage and actors remain, for the most part, unknown to both the public and law enforcement.

The victims of these frauds can be classified as either members of the private sector or members of the public sector. The former usually include consumers, businesses, and labor unions. Frauds involving consumers may take the form of Ponzi schemes, bait-and-switch tactics, repair and real estate swindles, and many others. To date, more than 800 consumer-related frauds have been identified.[9] A study of over 1000 individuals found that more than 60 percent of those sampled felt that they were consistently being sold shoddy products and had little or no faith in the marketplace.[10] They felt that no one really cared about the consuming public.

Not surprisingly, businesses are also victimized. They are the targets of bankruptcy frauds, phony insurance schemes, security frauds, thefts of products and valuable trade secrets, and computer and numerous other frauds. Law enforcement sources have identified approximately 500 frauds that victimize the business community.[11] Labor unions are also the targets of white-collar frauds. Their pension trusts have been raped, their treasuries robbed, and their membership employed to perpetrate numerous illegalities.

The public sector is also under attack, both at the local and national levels. These frauds usually take several forms; for example, they may involve government contracts or procurements, or various government programs. Vast Medicaid and Medicare frauds have surfaced, as well as schemes involving government subsidy and loan programs. These frauds exceed $10 billion annually; no one knows the exact figure, but all agree that the amounts suggested are extremely conservative. It should also be noted that these figures, when combined with those relating to frauds against the public sector, easily bring the cost of white-collar crime about $50 billion annually. For example, the cost of medical frauds alone is put at over $1 billion a year.[12] Neither the private nor the public sector is safe from this criminal onslaught.

The perpetrators of these frauds usually fall into one of three categories: (1) individuals, (2) businesses, and (3) organized crime. Frauds by individuals can be directed at both the private and public sectors. Technology, however, has given the individual tools that magnify his impact. For example, the computer enables an individual to steal millions of dollars at the push of a button.[13] New electronic interceptive tools enable an individual to steal valuable commercial and governmental data from great distances. Individuals have also been known to victimize insurance firms, government programs (for example, welfare, Medicare, Medicaid, social security, and employment compensation, which account for billions of lost dollars annually),[14] and the U.S. mail.

Businesses are often involved in predatory practices against smaller businesses. For example, price fixing and monopolistic schemes have destroyed many small firms. In one large Northeastern state, more than 1000 firms have been put out of business in the last several dozen years as a result of these practices.[15] Such price-fixing arrangements affect the economy in general and consumers in particular. In a recent case, four large firms were charged with fixing prices in the industrial porcelain area.[16] Food prices, housing costs, and almost all other facets of our economic system are, and have been, affected by these price-fixing and monopolistic arrangements. The public, and smaller firms, pay in terms of higher prices and decreased competition. Businesses are also involved in tax frauds, land swindles, charity schemes, tax violations, government contract frauds, and numerous other swindles.

Organized crime has come a long way since the roaring 1920s and the days of Al Capone. The heirs of the crime syndicates of the 1930s have now entered into the white-collar crime arena.[17] They have made their way into such areas as securities, real estate, home and auto repair schemes, as well as bankruptcy frauds, labor-related frauds, and many others. The days of the gangster carrying a machine gun in a violin case are gone; the new breed manipulates business, employs computers, and poses a serious threat to the public and private sectors.

Techniques of White-Collar Felons

All criminal endeavors have two characteristics: (1) an objective and (2) a modus operandi. Both traditional and white-collar crimes have these two features. However, they differ in that white-collar felons have grandiose objectives and, unfortunately, the ability to attain them. Whereas the traditional felon steals small sums of money, his nontraditional counterpart steals kingly sums. For example, the average bankrobber steals several thousand dollars; computer felons, however, steal more than $400,000 on the average. Some frauds have cost the public as much as $2 billion. With the advent of the cashless society (to be discussed later), the traditional felon may actually be a dying species.

The modus operandi of these two criminal classes also differs. Where the traditional felon uses brute force and crude tools, the white-collar criminal employs technology and mass communications and relies on the ignorance and greed of his victims. Naiveté and concealment play a key role in the arsenal of a white-collar felon. His victims, many times, are not even aware that they have been "taken" or harmed. Force and threats, however, are not totally absent from white-collar crimes. Organized criminals, when engaged in labor-related frauds or other nontraditional schemes, will often fall back on these primitive tools. Further, environmental crimes also tend to injure, maim, or destroy on a larger scale than the acts of the traditional felon. White-collar felons, unlike the less-educated, traditional felon, shy away from brute force, because the latter is largely ineffective and occasionally counterproductive. The tools and methods ultimately become a matter of rational choice. White-collar felons know that while juries and judges may forgive and forget the nonviolent theft of millions of dollars, they rarely forget physical harm inflicted on innocent victims.

The growing and impressive technology that we have unleashed in the last 30 years has given the white-collar felon the ability to further conceal and disguise his crimes. It has enabled him to steal large sums of money and property with impunity. For example, the likelihood of being uncovered in a computer crime is less than one in a hundred; the likelihood of being prosecuted for these frauds is also minimal; and if finally apprehended, the probability of going to prison is extremely remote. Little wonder, then, that these felons steal more than $40 billion a year.

Notes

1. Sid Feder and Joseph Dineen, "The Brinks Robbers," in *The Super Crooks*, Roger M. Williams, ed. (Chicago, Ill.: Playboy Press, 1973), pp. 163-164.

2. Peta Fordham, "The Great Train Robbers," in *The Super Crooks*, pp. 220-221.

3. Edwin H. Sutherland, "White Collar Criminality," in *White Collar Crime*, Gilbert Geis and Robert F. Meier, eds. (New York: Free Press, 1977), p. 42.

4. Clark Mollenhoff, "Billie Sol Estes," in *The Super Crooks*, p. 239; and see also, Ron Porambo, "An Autopsy of Newark," in *Theft of the City*, John A. Gardiner and David J. Olson, eds. (Bloomington, Indiana: Indiana Univ. Press, 1974), p. 87.

5. Clark Mollenhoff, "Billie Sol Estes," in *The Super Crooks*, p. 239.

6. A study by the U.S. Department of Commerce places the annual cost of white-collar crime at $30 billion; a study by the Chamber of Commerce of the United States places it at over $40 billion annually; and U.S. Senate sources place it at over $100 billion annually.

7. Based on interviews with prosecutors and investigators.

8. See Chamber of Commerce of the United States, *White Collar Crime* (Washington, D.C.: Chamber of Commerce of the United States, 1974), p. 6; see also, U.S. Department of Commerce, *Crime in Services Industries* (Washington, D.C.: Government Printing Office, 1977), pp. 3, 39, 95.

9. Chamber of Commerce of the United States, *White Collar Crime*, p. 26.

10. Louis Harris, "Many Americans Feel Quality of Life Is Worsening," *Washington Post*, November 21, 1977, p. A-3.

11. Based on interviews with both federal and private sources; one group of businessmen noted that coupon frauds alone accounted for between $100 million and $200 million in annual losses to the private business community.

12. Nancy Hicks, "Total of Medicare Fraud Put at $300 Million a Year," *New York Times*, July 29, 1977, p. 15; see also, Helen Dewar, "Medicaid Throwaway: One Billion a Year," *Washington Post*, October 17, 1977, p. A-1.

13. For a review of the problem of law enforcement and computer crime, see August Bequai, *Computer Crime* (Lexington, Mass.: Lexington Books, D.C. Heath, 1977), pp. 1-20.

14. "Compensation Frauds To Be Probed," *Washington Post,* November 21, 1977, p. A-7.

15. The New York State beer industry once had more than 1000 breweries within the state. Presently, it is controlled by a small number of giants. More than 900 breweries have disappeared as a result of predatory practices by these large national breweries.

16. "Four Firms Accept Order to Bar Fixing of Toilet Seat Prices," *Wall Street Journal,* August 12, 1977, p. 8.

17. New York State Commission of Investigation, *Racketeer Infiltration into Legitimate Business* (New York: New York State Commission of Investigations, 1970), pp. 37-49.

4 Securities-Related Crimes

The annual cost of securities-related crimes runs into the billions of dollars.[1] The total value of all stolen, missing, or counterfeit securities may run as high as $50 billion.[2] In 1974 a federal grand jury handed down a 24-count indictment charging the friend of a former United States President with conspiring to defraud one of the largest banks in the United States of $170 million.[3] That same year, federal investigators charged that an investment advisor had represented to his clients—reminiscent of the Middle Ages—that he would guarantee them high rates of return on their investments, because he had extrasensory perception.[4] It was also disclosed that a sixteen-year-old, who operated out of his bedroom in West Virginia, had been licensed as an investment advisor by the federal government.[5] A fifteen-year-old had been turned down only because he failed to forward a $150 application fee.[6]

Perhaps the most shocking news concerning the securities industry came in late August 1977. A federal report noted that the mayor of New York City, several officials, and a half dozen major financial institutions had misled investors in the offer, sale, and distribution of $4 billion of short-term city notes.[7] The investing public was not informed that the city might be unable to meet its financial obligations. Securities frauds present serious and extensive problems for law enforcement, in particular, and society as a whole.

Development of the Securities Industry

Financial frauds are not new, they can be traced back to ancient Egypt and Rome. In 1285 King Edward I of England gave the Court of Aldermen authority to police and regulate the growing brokerage industry in the City of London.[8] Prosecutions involving brokers were common before the year 1300.[9] During the sixteenth and seventeenth centuries, it was common for brokers and bankers to manipulate the prices of commodities and stocks. In 1697 Parliament enacted additional legislation to curb these abuses.[10]

The United States government, in an attempt to meet its war debts, issued $80 million in bonds in 1789.[11] Many of the states followed this example. In a short while, it became necessary to develop a forum in order to bring both buyers and sellers of securities together. In 1792 a group of New York stockbrokers met and signed the Buttonwood Tree Agreement, which

17

established the New York Stock Exchange (NYSE).[12] This exchange initially dealt in government securities, and those of a few banks and insurance companies. The exchange had no offices, and the meetings were held in the streets. About the same time, a group of Philadelphia stockbrokers established an exchange in their own city. In 1817 the NYSE adopted a constitution; members had to buy their seats. By 1886 the daily volume topped the 1 million mark.[13]

The American Stock Exchange (AMEX), the second largest exchange in this country, was founded in the mid-nineteenth century.[14] The exchange was first known as the Curb Exchange, and its members gathered in the streets of downtown New York City and conducted business in the open air. In 1953 it adopted its present name. The AMEX and the NYSE, together, handle about 80 percent of all stock transactions in this country.

Today there are more than a dozen other exchanges, which are known as the regional exchanges. At one time, there were more than 100 such markets. Of these secondary exchanges, the Pacific and Midwest are the most prominent. Another important market, the Over-the-Counter (OTC), has grown in the last several years and handles more than 10,000 issues.[15] This is the key market for government securities. Brokerage firms doing business in this market are usually known as "wholesalers," and their dealers play a key role in the OTC. All trading in the securities of publicly held corporations takes place in one or more of these exchanges.

In 1852 the state of Massachusetts passed legislation to curb much of the abuse that had grown in the securities industry. Many other states also enacted legislation in this area by 1908. Three years later the state of Kansas passed the first of the blue-sky laws. These statutes were later adopted by the majority of the states. Presently, most states have adopted what has come to be known as the Uniform Sale of Securities Act, which imposes criminal penalties on anyone who engages in securities frauds.[16] Many states also provide for licensing of individuals who are employed in the securities industry, and some jurisdictions allocate funds to provide for policing and regulation of this industry within their borders.

October 26, 1929 is known as Black Tuesday in the securities industry, the day of the notorious stock market debacle. It was apparent to many that, in large part, the crash had been caused by the lack of adequate disclosure of the true finances of publicly held corporations. In response to public pressure, the federal government enacted a series of laws, beginning with the Securities Act of 1933 (1933 Act). The U.S. Congress also established the Securities and Exchange Commission (SEC) in 1934 to police this area. The SEC was given authority to enact necessary rules and regulations for the securities industry, and also to enforce those regulations. In terms of enforcement, the SEC can: (1) take civil action, (2) take administrative action, and (3) refer the matter for criminal prosecution to the

Justice Department. The exchanges also have policing units within them, referred to as the "self-regulators." The SEC and these self-regulators police an industry that includes more than 6000 broker-dealers,[17] that employs more than 200,000 individuals,[18] and has assets of more than $500 billion.[19]

Securities Laws

Both state and federal securities laws have as their objective the licensing of individuals who are employed in the securities industry and the registration of any offering or the issuance of a security. They also seek to curb, and punish, the use of any device, scheme, or artifice to defraud, obtain money or property by false representations, or engage in any securities fraud. At the federal level, the SEC has jurisdiction over any transactions that affect interstate or foreign commerce. The states have jurisdiction over only those transactions that occur within their borders.

The ruling body of the SEC is known as the *Commission*. It is a quasi-judicial organ, composed of five members. Only three of these may belong to the same political party. The chairman of this body is selected by the President, with the advice and consent of the Senate. The SEC contains a number of divisions, the chief one being the Enforcement Division. This unit is the policing and prosecutorial organ of the SEC. It investigates all violations of the federal securities laws and brings these to the attention of the Commission. With the approval of the latter, it can then take civil or administrative action, and may also refer the investigatory files to the Justice Department for criminal prosecution. There are also nine regional offices and a number of branch offices that assist the Division of Enforcement in its policing role.

Section 2(1) of the 1933 Act defines a *security* as being any note, stock, treasury stock, bond, debenture, evidence of indebtedness, certificate of interest or participation in any profit-sharing agreement, investment contract, or, in general, any interest or instrument known as a security. The U.S. Supreme Court has defined it as being any investment of money: (1) in a common enterprise, (2) with the expectation of receiving profits, and (3) solely from the efforts of the promoter or a third party.[20] The courts have given the term *security* an extremely broad definition. It encompasses almost every type of investment of money where the investor does not contribute his labor, but relies rather on that of the promoter. Thus stocks, bonds, and even orange groves can constitute a security.

The key federal securities statutes are the 1933 Act and Securities Exchange Act of 1934 (1934 Act) The objectives of the 1933 Act are to: (1) provide investors with material, financial, and other data pertaining to the securities that are offered for sale to the public at large, and (2) to prohibit deceit, misrepresentation, and other fraudulent acts in the sale (not purchase) of securities. Section 5 of the 1933 Act provides that a registration statement must be filed with the SEC by the issuer (the firm selling the security), setting forth financial data on the issuing firm. The securities may not be sold until the registration statement has become effective, which usually takes 20 days after the filing. Until the effective date, it is unlawful to sell these securities. The act provides for criminal penalties and fines—imprisonment of up to five years and/or fines of up to $5,000—for a willful violation of the act.

The Commission, if petitioned, may advance the effective date, but this is discretionary with that body. In the registration statement, the issuer should describe the business, properties, capital, and management of the firm. The financial statements are certified by an independent accounting firm, purportedly to ensure their authenticity. False and misleading statements made in the registration statements are a violation of Section 17 of the act. Such statements may also be in violation of Sections 11 and 12 of the act. The objective of the registration provisions is to provide accurate and fair information for the investor to be able to make an educated assessment of the securities being offered for sale.[21] The SEC does not pass on the merits, value, or business viability of the firm in question. Prosecutions under the 1933 Act have covered such areas as fraud in the sale of securities, touting of stock, failure to register securities distributed in interstate commerce, and filing of false registration statements with the SEC.[22]

The federal registration requirements apply to both domestic and foreign securities being offered to the public for sale. Failure to abide by these requirements can be prosecuted criminally under Section 24 of the 1933 Act or civilly under Section 22. Frauds involving the sale of securities are prosecuted in this fashion. However, not all securities need be registered with the SEC because of certain exemptions. Criminals, in an attempt to evade the federal securities laws, attempt to bring the offering within one of these exemptions and thus evade filing a registration statement. Many frauds have been committed by simply evading a filing through one of these exemptions.

Key among these exemptions are private offerings to a limited number of individuals or institutions, provided, however, that the buyers are familiar with the corporation and thus have no need for written information in the form of a registration. In addition, these securities must not be redistributed. Thus individuals and institutions not familiar with the workings of the firm and therefore in need of additional data in the form of a writing will not be the purchasers of these securities. This is in line with the intent of the federal securities laws—only firms that make disclosure will be allowed to sell their securities to the public.

Securities that are sold within a state, do not affect interstate or foreign commerce, and do not employ the mails in their sale need not be registered with the SEC. However, they may have to be registered with the appropriate state agency. A failure to do so could result in prosecution by the state.

An offering of securities not exceeding $500,000 in amount may also be exempted from registration under Regulation A offerings. A Regulation A firm must, nevertheless, file a notification statement with the appropriate SEC regional office and must use an offering circular that contains information on the company (although not as indepth as in registration situations). The objective is to make it easier for small firms to sell their stocks to the public and to avoid the burden of a deluge of red tape. This laxity, however, allows criminal elements to take advantage of these exemptions and perpetrate numerous frauds. By the time the government acts, it is too late. For example, several years ago a small New York firm sold securities via the Regulation A vehicle. The New York SEC regional office reviewed the notification statement the firm had filed with it and allowed it to go through. A superficial review of the statements the firm filed with that office made it easy for the officers of the firm to fabricate information relating to the company. When the investigators were finally made aware of the fraud, it was too late. Stockholders had lost their money.[23]

In 1934, in an attempt to further extend the disclosure requirements on firms, the federal government enacted the Securities Exchange Act of 1934 (1934 Act). This act makes it a felony, punishable by up to two years imprisonment and/or up to $10,000 in fines, for anyone to:

1. employ any device, scheme, or artifice to defraud;
2. make any untrue statement of a material fact, or omit to state a material fact in order to make the statement made, in the light of the circumstances under which they were made, not misleading; or
3. engage in any act, practice, or course of business which operates or would operate as a fraud or deceit upon any person, in connection with the purchase or sale of any security.[24]

The act makes it a crime to falsely make, or omit to make, statements that are of a material nature and necessary for the investing public to make an educated assessment of securities. It also covers both the purchase and sale of securities, whereas the 1933 Act only covers purchases. Material falsities filed with the SEC will be prosecuted under the act. Omissions of a material nature, such as a company failing to disclose large sums of money used to bribe either domestic or foreign officials, will also be in violation of the act.

Numerous securities frauds have been prosecuted under the 1934 Act. For example, the manipulation of the market in listed securities is a violation, as well as any fraud in either the purchase or sale of securities. The falsification of any filings, annual reports, or any registration statement is also a violation of the 1934 Act. The 1933 Act could possibly be employed here as well. False filings by members of the brokerage industry will also be in violation, along with trading in securities on "inside information" (to be covered later in the chapter).

There are several other securities acts that should be mentioned in any discussion of securities regulation. For example, the 1935 Act requires officers and controlling shareholders of registered public holding companies to report their ownership of securities; the 1940 Act covers the investment industry; and the 1940 Advisors Act covers investment advisors. Several other statutes have also been enacted. However, except for the 1933 and 1934 Acts, the other statutes play a minor enforcement role. Prosecutions under these other statutes, when combined, count for fewer than a dozen criminal prosecutions. Criminal cases brought under the 1933 and 1934 Acts account for the bulk of prosecutions for securities frauds.

Understanding the Corporate Animal

We have been conditioned to think of a corporation as an entity with its own personality and unique behavior. For example, some companies are known as "bad," while others have a reputation for being "good." Recently, one businessman proposed that we rehabilitate the bad ones, as if they were human and could be salvaged through therapy. There is, for example, the case of a large Buffalo-based corporation that operates in several foreign countries and in 39 states within this country.[25] It owns race tracks and professional sports teams and grosses more than $500 million annually. In 1972 a Los Angeles grand jury brought an indictment against the firm that resulted in a subsequent conviction. Five years later, the firm petitioned the President of the United States to pardon it. Prominent political figures also threw their weight behind this move. Lawyers for the company argued that it had radically altered its behavior and deserved leniency. It had, they said, changed its ways. The petition was denied.

Corporations, in the eyes of the law, are entities with legal rights, separate and distinct from those of the people who own or manage them. They are creatures of the police power of the state. Their charter, or articles of incorporation, gives them birth. They are usually classified as being either private or public. The former is established by private interest for the purpose of commerce of finance; the latter is established to serve a governmental need. A third type of corporate entity is the quasi-public one. This is usually a private interest serving a public need. Public utilities are examples of this type of corporation.

The formation of this artificial person is a simple matter. In most jurisdictions, three or more individuals may apply for a corporate charter and file proposed articles of incorporation with the state. The simplicity with which it can be established, and the legal identity of the corporate entity, offers felons a vehicle and veil behind which they can sometimes disguise their activities. The application lists the name of the proposed entity, its objectives, place of business, duration, officers, directors (at least three), incorporators, and capital stock. Most jurisdictions require that a corporate entity not commence doing business until at least $1000 has been received from the sale of its shares.

The corporate entity has a continuous life, regardless of who its stockholders are. It can borrow money or enter into contracts with other corporate entities or individuals. It can issue or endorse negotiable instruments, can transfer and purchase property, and can issue bonds and stock. Some corporations sell their securities to the public at large and do this through one of the exchanges already discussed. In the process, they file statements (registration) with the appropriate federal and/or state agencies.[26]

Corporations issue two types of stock: (1) common and (2) preferred. The former entitles a shareholder to one vote for each share owned. (The shareholder is also entitled to share in the profits of the firm in the form of dividends.) The latter category of stock has priority over common stock with respect to dividends. It may also have priority over common in the distribution of capital upon dissolution of the firm. Both common and preferred stock, in the case of publicly traded corporations, sell in one or more of the exchanges. The sale, purchase, offer, and other related matters in the instance of these publicly traded securities are controlled and dictated by both state blue-sky laws and the federal securities laws. The intent of these laws is to protect the public at large, which has limited or no knowledge of the corporate entity. Disclosure, to the investor, is a key factor in his decisionmaking. It is one's perception of the company and its finances that leads to investment in that firm's securities. Felons attempt to distort this perception through either the release of false information and/or the omission of material information.

Recently, one of the largest oil firms in this country was charged by the government with violating the federal securities laws. The firm had set up secret Swiss bank accounts and used these to funnel bribes to foreign political leaders.[27] A large car-rental firm disclosed that it had made more than $400,000 in questionable foreign payments.[28] In a separate case, the government accused an invention-promotional firm of evading the securities registration laws.[29] Several thousand investors had gone to this firm with their ideas. The firm, in turn, promised to evaluate, promote, and patent their ideas for a fee of $1000. These agreements were known as "development contracts." The government, however, maintained that the firm's agreements were securities and should have been registered with it.

The preceding cases illustrate one elemental truth of the business world: management and not the shareholders run the everyday affairs of a company. Large shareholders may have a stronger voice; but within a large corporate framework, the everyday affairs are too numerous and tedious for any one shareholder to deal with properly. Shareholders do have certain rights; they can inspect corporate books and records. However, because of the necessary technical know-how and the voluminous records involved in a large firm, the shareholder relies on what management tells him or her about the firm. It is precisely because of this that state and federal laws place such great stress on the disclosure of the firm's finances. A shareholder may sue, on behalf of the corporation, either management or its directors for damages caused by their wrongdoing. The shareholder's liabilities, however, are limited. He is not personally liable for the corporation's debts or wrongdoing. His risk is limited to the original capital he invested, although shareholders are the legal owners of the corporation. Management, with the growing complex nature of the business world, has assumed greater control and, in some instances, has perpetrated great abuse.

The management of a firm is entrusted, at least theoretically, to the board of directors. Board members are elected by the shareholders of the company. Many directors sit on several corporate boards, giving rise to legitimate fears that the confidential information they acquire in their duties as board members may be used for private investment purposes—buying based on inside information. The board of directors, especially where the directors are either the founders or large stockholders in a firm, can exercise great powers. Abuse is also a very real concern. For example, in the early 1970s, the board of a large firm made it an informal policy for the firm to show a steady 15 percent growth rate. Profit-and-loss records were altered; there was an attempt to dupe even the auditors of the firm.[30] In another case, one director and the chief executive officer of a firm were accused by government investigators of altering company records. The alteration was an attempt to disguise more than $4 million in illegal payments made to customers of the firm in order to obtain and retain their good will.[31] In a third case, former high company officials were accused by the government of altering, inflating, and creating fictitious sales and inventory to funnel millions of dollars of company money for their own personal benefit.[32]

In most organizations, the board of directors is the titular manager of the firm, and everyday affairs are actually conducted by management. The board usually delegates its managerial obligations to company officers. Some directors may also serve as high company officials. As agents of the company, officers are limited in their authority by the charter and bylaws of the company, as well as by the laws of agency. The board also issues instructions and supervises overall activities. However, with disclosures of managerial abuse in recent years, boards have come under increasing attack for having abandoned the firm to management. The relationship of company officials to the firm is a fiduciary one. They are liable, under law, for personal profits made at the expense of the firm; and they are also liable for willful or negligent actions that cause a loss to the firm. They are not, however, liable for everyday errors, provided there was no imprudent business conduct. The personality and everyday behavior of a firm must be accredited, in large part, to management's own conduct and also to that of the board of directors.

The personality and everyday behavior of a corporation reflects the relationship between management and its board; this relationship determines the corporation's course and fortune; management and the board set and implement policy. The stockholders, especially in large corporations, are innocent bystanders. They depend on the federal and state securities laws to ensure that their investments will not fall prey to fraud. Unfortunately, this has not been the case. Even the more sophisticated stockholders, as many recent frauds have demonstrated, can fall victim to securities-related crimes. Several years ago, investors lost more than $200 million to a massive securities fraud.[33] The chairman and president of the firm personally gained $10 million. Among those who lost their investments were many well-known financial institutions. The president of the firm was sentenced to one year imprisonment, but became eligible for parole within four months. He received no fines.

Categories of Offenses

Securities-related offenses take on various forms. One of the more common involves blue-sky law violations. States have their own securities laws that attempt to regulate the offer, sale, purchase, and registration of securities sold intrastate. These laws provide for both civil and criminal penalties.

Churning, a common abuse of stock brokers, involves short-term trading swings by brokers, especially when the client has given them discretionary powers over his account. The objective of churning is to generate huge commissions for the broker. The latter earns his livelihood through client commissions and thus has a vested interest in encouraging short-term buying and selling. The client, either relying on his broker's judgment and decisionmaking or else on his broker's advice, will participate in this without fully realizing the ultimate effect upon him. By the time he becomes aware of what is happening, he may have lost large sums of money and the broker will probably have gained huge commissions. Churning is a violation of the federal securities laws.

Unauthorized trading by brokers in a client's account is illegal. The broker, although not given power of attorney over a client's account, nevertheless takes the liberty to trade occasionally. Although a violation of law, brokers sometimes give the excuse that they acted on oral instructions from their clients. Since it is the broker's word against that of his client, prosecution is usually difficult.

Trading on inside information is another of the more common securities violations. Typically, a broker will use nonpublic information to an unfair advantage for himself or his clients over the other shareholders of the company. Trading on inside information may also involve company executives or directors who have access to confidential financial information. Based on such information, they may either buy or sell stock to their own advantage. The end result is that the public suffers not only a financial loss, but also a loss of confidence in the market place.

The classic insider-trading case involved the Texas Gulf Sulphur Company.[34] In November 1963, engineers for the company had drilled a test hole to determine if a certain area contained substantial amounts of copper and zinc. It was soon discovered that in fact large deposits lay buried in this region. No public announcement was made of the find. In 1964 additional tests were run, and there was further confirmation that in fact this area was rich in copper and zinc. While the information was still confidential and restricted to a small group within the company, some of its employees purchased additional shares in the company's stock. The SEC brought civil suit, and the court held that these purchases were illegal and in violation of the securities laws.[35] The court further added that all investors should have equal access to material information.[36] In essence, the court said that company officials (insiders) should not have an advantage over the public at large in the trading of company securities. The test of materiality is what an average investor would consider reasonably necessary to make a prudent decision on whether to buy or sell securities.[37]

Manipulation of stock is also a common offense. A broker who has a vested interest in a stock may make false or misleading statements to his clients or members of the general public, either directly or indirectly, with the objective of creating an artificial demand for the stock. He may be assisted by company officials, other brokers, or even members of the general financial community. The false information may be disseminated in the form of a press release, market analyst report, etc. The end result is that the stock is made to appear much more desirable than it really is. According to government investigators, one victim had been told by his broker that his stock would be "the next IBM." The victim invested and lost thousands of dollars. The firm was on the verge of bankruptcy and the broker wanted to unload his stock and that of his friends on an uninformed public.[38]

Boiler-room operations are also common in the securities industry. A number of manipulators will, through hard-sell tactics and a barrage of false or misleading information, induce members of the uninformed public to invest in unknown companies whose stock may be worth little, if anything. The buyer is led to believe that the company will do well. Once the manipulators unload the stock, the investor is left holding the bag.

One of the better known and more common securities frauds is the *Ponzi scheme*, named after Charles Ponzi who first initiated it in 1920. Ponzi's gimmick was Spanish postal reply coupons, which sold in Europe for 1 cent and could be redeemed in the United States for 10 cents. Ponzi promised investors a 50 percent return on their investment within a two-month period. More than 40,000 people invested more than $10 million in these Spanish postal coupons and waited for their enormous gains, as Ponzi had promised. No one bothered to check with the Spanish authorities if in fact such coupons had ever been issued and, if so, in what amounts. It was later learned that fewer than $1 million in these coupons had been issued by the Spanish government and that Ponzi had misled his investors. He was subsequently prosecuted and imprisoned.

Many years later, in the Commonwealth of Virginia, an employee of the Chesapeake & Potomac Telephone Company promised hundreds of investors 30 to 100 percent returns on their investments if they bought promissory notes in his European "industrial wine" scheme. A number of banks and prominent Virginia businessmen and political figures invested several million dollars in this "get rich quick" scheme. When investigators uncovered the fraud, some 400 investors had lost over $20 million.[39]

In a more recent case, more than 1000 airline pilots stand to lose as much as $40 million in a classic Ponzi scheme. The mastermind of this alleged fraud is a Los Angeles lawyer who promised large returns in tax-shelter ventures to thousands of investors.[40] The latter were barraged with telephone calls and mass mailings; many fell for the scheme.

In the early 1960s, American investors discovered off-shore banks. One of the better known off-shore bank frauds involved the notorious Bank of Sark. The bank was located on an English island, from which it took its name. Bank officials represented the bank as having assets of over $70 million. Bank of Sark certificates of deposit and letters of credit were widely sold to criminal elements, who in turn used them to defraud investors out of more than $40 million. The bank became a base of operation for organized crime figures. These phony letters of credit and certificates of deposit were used to acquire control of legitimate businesses.

Stolen and counterfeit securities run in the billions of dollars. In one New York brokerage firm, a well-organized ring was said to be stealing several million dollars worth of securities monthly.[41] One gang, when caught, was said to have more than $10 million in counterfeit securities in its possession.[42] Recently, a Pakistani citizen was indicted for using altered stock certificate specimens as collateral for bank loans.[43] The defendant would visit printers who had samples of stock certificates and ask to see some. He would then take the samples with him, telling the printers he wanted to review them with his associates. He would erase the word *specimen* and pass them on to unsuspecting bankers. In July 1977, the SEC initiated an experimental project—Autex—to gather and computerize information on stolen securities. The data bank would make this information available to banks and other financial institutions, hopefully to assist them in detecting stolen and counterfeit securities. The project, however, is too new for a present evaluation of its effectiveness to be made. Critics charge that the effort is too little and too late.

Banks and brokerage firms, however, have been reluctant to take any action to curb thefts and counterfeit operations that bilk them and the public of billions of dollars. (For many years, they were even opposed to project Autex.) A similar, privately funded system has been in operation for several years. The basis for resisting such projects is the holder-in-due-course doctrine. This law reinforces the reluctance to institute security measures because under this doctrine, one who takes an instrument (stocks or bonds) and who: (1) pays or gives something of value for it (a bank may give a loan for it if it holds it as collateral), (2) does so in good faith, and (3) has no notice that there is a claim on it by another party (the original owner of the securities) or any other defect in the instrument (that it is counterfeit) is not liable and is a holder in good stead. If the counterfeit or stolen instrument is discovered by another party, the bank or brokerage firm cannot be held liable, since it believed in good faith that the instrument was genuine. The problem is proving that the party did not have a good faith belief, that in fact it shut its eyes. Organized crime has wreaked havoc in this area.

Securities Cops

The SEC can take one or more of the following three actions against a violator of the securities laws: (1) administrative, (2) civil, and (3) criminal referral to the Justice Department. In the first instance, the defendant may be barred from the industry or suspended for a period of time. There are no fines or criminal penalties. For example, an investment advisor who used false or misleading advertising to induce the public to turn to his services was only censured by the SEC.[44] The defendant agreed to the action without admitting to the charges. Those who lost their money could not use the censure as an admission of guilt by the defendant in a court of law; in turn, the defendant escaped prolonged discovery and litigation.

In the area of civil action, more than 90 percent of all SEC cases result in consent agreements. The latter is a contract between the defendant and the government, whereby the former promises to abide by the law and the latter promises not to prosecute for the present violations. However, the defendant does not admit any guilt. If the defendant chooses to litigate the matter, the SEC may eventually obtain an injunction. The latter, however, is only an order to the defendant to cease and desist from further fraudulent activity. It is not retroactive, and many defendants keep the proceeds of their illicit activities.

Criminal referrals are rare, and criminal prosecutions are almost nonexistent. Fewer than 5 percent of all SEC investigations culminate in such prosecutions.[45] Criminal cases are extremely time consuming, litigation may be extensive, and it may be several years before a verdict is finally handed down. Further, the likelihood of imprisonment is only 21.5 percent, according to a study by the Bureau of National Affairs.[46] As a result, many investigators and prosecutors, when possible, take the consent-decree route. One federal prosecutor noted that, "it's not worth spending years on a case only to have the fellow walk out on probation." The truth of such a sentiment is self-evident.

The stock exchanges have their own private investigatory forces. These regulatory divisions are staffed by both attorneys and investigators. The NYSE spends several million dollars annually on regulatory activities, as does the AMEX.[47] These self-regulators are valuable policing tools and can be of assistance to federal law enforcement. For example, in one recent case, three brokerage firms were expelled by the National Association of Securities Dealers after it was found that they had violated the securities laws.

However, the self-regulators are seriously overworked; complaints are often registered that the SEC has failed to provide adequate support. From 1974 through 1976, the self-regulators referred more than 180 cases to the SEC for action; fewer than 1 out of 60 resulted in any court action.[48] The exchanges themselves suffer from a maze of bureaucratic red tape. Complaints involving member firms are referred to a committee, which acts as a quasi-judicial body. Its decisions can be appealed to the Board of Governors of the exchange. The process is time consuming, and cases can take several years before a final decision is handed down. The outcome may be a fine or suspension. Expulsion is rare and usually involves only extreme cases that should have been prosecuted criminally in the first place.

The securities enforcers are handicapped by a flood of red tape, as well as by the very complex nature of securities frauds. Further, a maze of antiquated rules and regulations invites criminal activity. For example, a thirteen-year-old can apply for registration as an investment advisor, and the SEC's staff can do little to keep him or her out. In addition, some sectors of the securities industry, in their attempts to curtail regulation, have castrated the normal law enforcement role that the securities enforcers can play. At present, the public is victimized for billions of dollars annually.

Notes

1. Chamber of Commerce of the United States, *White Collar Crime* (Washington, D.C.: Chamber of Commerce of the United States, 1974), p. 6.

2. Ibid., p. 48.

3. Public Citizens Staff Report, *White Collar Crime* (Washington, D.C.: Congress Watch, 1974), p. 10.

4. Jack Anderson, "Investment Advisers: Even Teenagers Get Licenses," *Washington Post*, August 15, 1976, p. C-7.

5. Ibid.

6. Ibid.

7. "SEC Weighs Action After Its Staff Accuses City, Banks of Hiding New York's Plight," *Wall Street Journal*, August 29, 1977, p. 2.

8. David E. Spray, ed., *The Principal Stock Exchanges of the World* (Washington, D.C.: International Economic Publishers, 1964), p. 16.

9. Ibid.

10. Ibid.

11. Ibid., p. 3.

12. Ibid., p. 4.

13. Ibid., p. 5.

14. Ibid., p. 21.

15. Ibid.; see also U.S., Securities and Exchange Commission, *Annual Report for 1975* (Washington, D.C.: Government Printing Office, 1975), pp. 76-78.

16. Ronald A. Anderson and Walter A. Kumpf, *Business Law* (Chicago, Ill.: Southwestern, 1967), p. 753.

17. U.S. Securities and Exchange Commission, *Annual Report for 1976* (Washington, D.C.: Government Printing Office, 1976), p. 180.

18. Ibid.

19. Ibid., p. 197.

20. *Securities and Exchange Commission* v. *Howey*, 328 U.S. 293 (1946).

21. Hill and Knowlton, Financial Relations Unit, *The SEC, the Stock Exchanges and Your Financial Public Relations* (New York: Hill & Knowlton, 1972), pp. 40-41.

22. Arthur F. Mathews and William P. Sullivan, "Criminal Liability for Violations of the Federal Securities Laws: The National Commission's Proposed Federal Criminal Code, S.1 and S.1400," *The American Criminal Law Rev.*XI (1973):883.

23. Based on my experience as a former federal prosecutor.

24. 17 C.F.R. sec. 240.10b-5, and 15 U.S.C. 78j(b).

25. Bill Richards, "Corporation Seeks Compassion," *Washington Post*, August 29, 1977, p. A-3.

26. For a review of the legal powers of a corporation, see Harry G.

Henn, *Handbook of the Law of Corporations and Other Business Enterprises* (St. Paul, Minn.: West, 1970), pp. 107-131.

27. John F. Berry, "SEC Charges Oil Firm with Hiding Foreign Revenues," *Washington Post*, May 4, 1977, p. C-1.

28. Ibid.

29. "SEC Cites Invention Promoters for $4 Million Fraud Scheme," *Washington Post*, August 9, 1977, p. D-8.

30. Based on my experiences while employed at the Securities and Exchange Commission.

31. "Arden-Mayfair, Two Aides Are Charged by SEC with Fraud and False Reporting," *Washington Post*, August 19, 1977, p. 34.

32. Based on my experiences while employed at the Securities and Exchange Commission.

33. Public Citizen Staff Report, *White Collar Crime* (Washington, D.C.: Congress Watch, 1974), pp. 11, 12.

34. Hill and Knowlton, Financial Relations Unit, *The SEC, the Stock Exchanges and Your Financial Public Relations*, pp. 9, 10.

35. Ibid., p. 11.

36. Ibid.

37. Ibid., p. 13

38. Based on my interviews with federal officials.

39. "Charles Ponzi's Legacy," *Business Week*, June 29, 1974, p. 61.

40. Jim Drinkhall, "Thousands of Investors Accuse California Man of Defrauding Them," *Wall Street Journal*, April 22, 1977, p. 1.

41. Chamber of Commerce of the United States, *White Collar Crime*, p. 48.

42. Ibid., p. 49.

43. "Pakistani Is Indicted for Securities Fraud Believed To Be Novel," *Wall Street Journal*, August 18, 1977, p. 26.

44. "Investment Adviser is Censured by SEC for Misleading Ads," *Wall Street Journal*, August 12, 1977, p. 4.

45. U.S. Securities and Exchange Commission, *Annual Report for 1975*, pp. 209, 210.

46. John A. Jenkins and Robert H. Rhode, *White Collar Justice Special Report* (Washington, D.C.: Bureau of National Affairs, 1976), p. 11.

47. John A. Jenkins, "Flood of Insider Trading Referrals to SEC Result in Trickle of Investigations, Lawsuits," *Bureau of National Affairs Securities Regulation & Law Reports*, July 20, 1977, p. A-4; and John A. Jenkins, "The Self-Regulators," *Bureau of National Affairs Securities Regulation & Law Reports*, April 20, 1977, pp. AA-8, AA-9.

48. Ibid.; see also, John A. Jenkins, "Securities Enforcement: A Growth Industry, the Critics," *Bureau of National Affairs Securities Regulation & Law Reports,* April 13, 1977, p. AA-1; and John A. Jenkins, "In Case of Corruption, Break Glass," *Student Lawyer* (November 1977): 39.

Bankruptcy Frauds

The Merkel Meat Company had an excellent reputation in New York's meat industry.[1] The old owners sold the firm to a group of buyers. The new owner, taking advantage of the firm's good name in the business community, began to substitute the quality line of meat products with an inferior one. Meats never intended for human consumption were incorporated into the firm's frankfurters. Investigators later discovered that the meat of dead and dying animals, ordinarily used as mink meat, was sold to the public. The new owners also began to run high debts. Eventually, the company went into bankruptcy. Creditors lost millions of dollars, and the public had ingested meat that had never been designated for human consumption.

The preceding serves to illustrate the serious and ever-increasing problem of bankruptcy fraud, also known as "scams," "bust-outs," or "planned bankruptcies."[2] The annual loss due to bankruptcy fraud exceeds $50 million.[3] The crime thus touches every facet of our economy, and many firms have already fallen victim. Felons have taken advantage of our legal framework to bilk both business and the public. In a credit-oriented society, bankruptcy frauds represent not only a menace to our economic well-being, but also a threat to the legitimacy of our financial structures. Not surprisingly, organized criminal elements have also made their way into this area.

Bankruptcy Laws

Bankruptcy is defined as a proceeding that deals with the property and obligations of an insolvent debtor and his creditors. Under the federal framework, the Constitution has conferred power on the U.S. Congress to establish a uniform system of laws on the "subject of bankruptcies."[4] Various states have laws that address, in one form or other, the problem of bankruptcy. However, matters involving bankruptcy are generally handled by federal district courts.

With the growth of the business community, the federal government began to take a greater interest in the area of bankruptcy. The federal bankruptcy law—also known as the Chandler Act of 1938—contains 15 chapters. The first 7 chapters deal with the traditional forms of bankruptcy. These usually revolve around the discharge of an honest bankrupt. The latter chapters deal with the problem of rehabilitating the debtor. One of the more significant provisions is Chapter 10, which deals with corporate reorganization.

Bankruptcy proceedings can be: (1) voluntary or (2) involuntary. Voluntary proceedings are usually commenced by the debtor, who may be any person, including a corporation. However, municipal, railroad, insurance, and banking institutions are not qualified as a person within the bankruptcy laws. (For example, railroads are covered by the Transportation Act and fall within the jurisdiction of the Interstate Commerce Commission.) Involuntary proceedings are commenced by a creditor or creditors, and any natural person, business, or commercial corporate entity may become involuntarily bankrupt. Municipal, railroad, insurance, and banking institutions are the exception once again.

Since the scam (bankruptcy fraud) involves the involuntary bankruptcy of a firm by its creditors, it is important to further explore these proceedings. In voluntary bankruptcy, an individual or firm files a petition with the local federal district court declaring bankruptcy. This is an automatic adjudication that the debtor is bankrupt. The petitioner must file an inventory of all his property and a list of all his creditors, showing the amount owed each. The petitioner must also file a statement of affairs, which details financial transactions, volume of business (if it is a corporate entity), and income.

The court usually refers bankruptcy matters to a referee-in-bankruptcy. The referee fixes a date for the meeting of the creditors, which is usually not less than 10 days nor more than 30 days after adjudication of the petitioner in bankruptcy. The bankrupt is required to attend this meeting and be examined by the creditors or their attorneys. At their first meeting, the creditors elect a trustee-in-bankruptcy, who is usually a local attorney. It is his responsibility to gather all the assets of the bankrupt and, implicitly, to uncover any frauds. The adjudication of a corporate petitioner as a bankrupt will not release its officers, directors, and even shareholders from any liability under law.[5] After administrative costs are paid, any remaining assets are distributed among the creditors.[6]

The bankruptcy laws provide for five classes of claims that are entitled to priority on distribution. All creditors are required to submit with the court a proof of claim, in writing and signed. These claims must be filed within six months after the first date set for the meeting of the creditors and must be allowed unless challenged by one of the parties who has an interest in the matter.[7]

Claimants are paid in order of priority. Those in a lower priority are not paid until everyone in the higher classes has been paid. Administrative costs have the highest priority and include the fees of the trustee, the attorney for the petitioner, the petitioning creditors, and others connected with the administration of the bankrupt's estate. Wage claims up to $600 earned within three months are next in line. These are followed by costs and expenses of creditors incurred in successfully opposing the discharge or in presenting evidence that led to a conviction of the bankrupt for bankruptcy fraud. Federal, state, and local taxes are the fourth priority; other debts form the fifth class.

In an involuntary bankruptcy proceeding, the creditors and not the debtor initiate the process. Although, once the process is commenced, it differs little from that of a voluntary proceeding, the factors behind the initiation of the process are somewhat different. The creditors must allege that an act of bankruptcy was committed by the debtor within four months prior to the filing of their petition.[8] An act may take the form of a fraudulent removal, transfer, or concealment of property, which is the usual procedure in a scam operation. There are various other acts that can also rise to an involuntary bankruptcy proceeding. For example, the debtor appears to be engaged in preferential transfers of his property. An admission in writing of inability to pay debts and of willingness to be adjudicated bankrupt can also give rise to the creditors' action. In bankruptcy fraud situations, where the felons have bilked the firm of its property, creditors are forced to embark on this course. On their shoulders and that of the trustee, falls the difficult task of unraveling the fraud.

If the debtor has more than 12 creditors, at least 3 of these must initiate the involuntary proceedings. If there are less than 12 creditors, 1 creditor can initiate the process. The petitioners, however, must have claims aggregating $500; the debtor must owe at least $1000. Further, the debtor must be insolvent at the time of the commission of the bankruptcy act. The burden of establishing insolvency is on the creditors, and mere suspicion is not sufficient. In part, this explains why creditors are not able to act with requisite speed when they suspect a scam operation. The debtor has a right to a jury trial, if he so requests, on the issue of insolvency.

The bankrupt's primary concern is the discharge of his debts. Under the law, he is entitled to a discharge unless proper objections are raised and sustained. In the case of individuals, adjudication operates as an automatic application for discharge. A defunct corporation usually goes out of business regardless, and need not apply for discharge. Corporations, however, must file an application for discharge within six months of adjudication.

Once filed, a discharge is usually granted, unless it can be shown that the bankrupt has violated the bankruptcy criminal statutes. Section 152, Title 18, of the United States Code makes it a felony (punishable by up to 5 years imprisonment and/or up to $5000 in fines) for anyone to fraudulently transfer property of a corporation that is in contemplation of bankruptcy. The proposed revision to the Federal Criminal Code (S.1437 and H.R.3907) retains this clause, with some minor modifications.

The unjustifiable destruction of books and records can also negate a discharge. The obtaining of money or credit, while in business, based on false financial statements, the refusal to obey lawful orders of the courts, a failure to explain losses or deficiencies of assets, the transfer within one year prior to bankruptcy of assets with intent to defraud one's creditors, and the granting of a discharge in bankruptcy within six years prior to the filing of the present petition will block a discharge.

The problem with bankruptcy frauds is that creditors and the trustee in the case are expected to act as investigators. The burden of proving the fraud, at least initially, is placed on their shoulders. This is no easy task, since many scams are perpetrated by sophisticated felons and, in some instances, by organized criminal rings. Creditors are usually spread out over several states and lack the investigatory expertise to handle white-collar crime investigations. If they retain counsel, it means that they must bear this added financial burden. Further, the trustee, usually a local attorney, has no criminal investigatory experience; he is neither trained nor armed with the necessary resources to conduct a successful investigation. Complex frauds are particularly difficult to unravel. Even if the creditors and trustee uncover a fraud, the felon faces civil rather than criminal charges.

Section 2516(e), Title 18, of the United States Code empowers federal authorities to apply to a local federal judge for an order authorizing a wiretap in cases involving a bankruptcy fraud. Section 3057 provides that a referee or trustee who has reasonable grounds to believe that a bankruptcy fraud has taken place can refer the matter to local federal prosecutors. These two sections, at least on the surface, appear to give the federal authorities the requisite muscle to act. However, in practice, federal prosecutors have been slow to act and usually shy away from complex bankruptcy frauds. Further, federal prosecutors rely on the investigatory apparatus to prepare their cases for trial. In most instances, referees and trustees are ill prepared to do this.

Local prosecutors can also act in cases involving a scam by employing the false-pretense statutes. This crime consists of five elements: (1) a false representation of a material present or past fact, (2) which causes the victim, (3) to pass title to, (4) his property to the wrongdoer, (5) who knows his representation to be false and intends thereby to defraud the victim. The problem local prosecutors face in bankruptcy fraud cases is that in many instances the frauds are interstate in nature and their own jurisdiction is limited. Suspects and witnesses may be living in other states, and it may be difficult to locate them and more difficult to bring them within the locality. Further, local prosecutors in many cases do not have the large sums of money needed to prosecute these complex frauds. Small budgets and ill-trained staffs are a barrier to successful prosecution. In addition, the prosecutor must show beyond a reasonable doubt that the defendant intended to defraud his creditors. This is often no easy task. Various defenses are usually raised in such cases. They range from "I only made a business judgment" to a variety of other explanations, such as the goods were shipped late by the creditor or were in some defective condition. In one such fraud, the defendant noted,

When I received the merchandise and found something wrong with it, I would call. . . . I told them what was wrong. There is many times they didn't believe me. . . . There were many times they would not give me the allowance so I would send the merchandise back, and this happened many, many times. . . . At any price, I didn't want it. . . . They would not give me any credits.[9]

The bankruptcy laws were initially enacted to protect the innocent bankrupt. However, the great expansion of credit and the enhanced sophistication of our criminal class have enabled that class to take advantage of the loopholes of these laws. Creditors are expected to uncover sophisticated frauds that may occasionally employ the most recent technology—the computer. Trustees are asked to police and detect frauds, when in fact they lack the requisite training, as well as the needed resources. Local attorneys have numerous commitments, and it is unrealistic to expect a private member of the bar to unravel sophisticated frauds, since the demands of such an undertaking are beyond his means. Prosecutors have shown a reluctance to tackle this difficult arena. One prosecutor noted, in confidence, that there is no "percentage in handling one case when you can handle many."

Categories of Scams

Bankruptcy frauds are found in most industries. Businesses that handle merchandise with a high turnover potential are usually more attractive to such felons. The goods are readily disposed of and are difficult for the police to trace. However, bankruptcy frauds usually fall into one or more of the following four categories: (1) the "similar name" scam, (2) the "old" company technique, (3) the "new" company technique, and (4) the "successful business" scam.

The *similar-name scam* usually involves the formation of a company with a name similar to an older established firm. The idea is to mislead suppliers into believing that the new firm is in fact the older and more established one. The felons attempt to portray their firm as being connected with the older one. Since state law requires that a new corporation not use the same name of an existing firm, the felons attempt to approximate the identity of the older firm as much as possible.

Once having established this similar-name entity, the felons embark on a buying program. Large orders are placed with numerous suppliers, especially those who are out-of-state and find it more difficult to check the authenticity of this new firm; the suppliers have little reason to suspect a fraud. Should they eventually suspect a scam, they are already fully committed and do not want to upset the cart. The felons will usually sell the merchandise to either legitimate or illegitimate sources. Fences obviously play a significant part in this process. At the same time, the felons bilk their corporate entity of its assets and eventually file for bankruptcy (voluntary) or wait until the creditors commence these proceedings (involuntary), once the latter discover the degree of the fraud. By the time that a trustee is appointed, the felons will have either flown the coop or erased their tracks, making the impending inquiry a difficult matter.

A second technique is the *old-company scam*. An established firm, which has operated in a city for many years, decides to make quick profits. In part, this may be motivated by loss of business revenue or by outside intervention. For example, the firm may have taken on new partners in the form of organized crime figures. Several years ago, a large New York meat wholesaler was infiltrated by organized crime. Within a short period of time, suppliers lost more than $1 million to this scam. The old owners, finding themselves in financial difficulties, had taken silent partners.

The *new-company scam* is a third technique often used by felons. A new company is formed, and a front man is made its executive officer. Unlike his partners, he may have no prior criminal record and will not raise any suspicions. Credit is established, and a large or plush office may be rented. Large orders are soon placed with numerous suppliers. During the first months of operation, the orders are usually small but become progressively larger. Once received, the merchandise is converted into cash, usually with the assistance of a large fence. The company is eventually forced into involuntary bankruptcy by its creditors, but by this time all funds have been transferred out of it by the operators.

In the late 1960s, a large and well-established pharmaceutical firm fell victim to a fourth type of scam—the *successful-business scam*. The firm had sales of approximately $10 million, and employed 10 salesmen and a staff of about 90 people who ran its warehouse.[10] When the founder of the company died, new owners assumed control of the corporation. Within a short period of time, the firm was bilked of more than $500,000. Stockholders and suppliers suffered the entire loss.

This last scam resembles the other three in that large orders are placed with suppliers and no notice of change in management is given the suppliers. Merchandise, once received, is sold to either legitimate or illegitimate sources. The funds are milked out of the company, and the firm soon goes into bankruptcy. The creditors stand little chance of recouping their losses, and the felons stand an excellent chance of evading prosecution.

The Role of Fences

Scam operators find an outlet for their merchandise either through the legitimate sector—firms and individuals who are not aware of the scam—or through a series of fences. The latter play the role of middlemen, bringing supply and demand together.[11] Without the assistance of fences, scam operators might have a more difficult time selling their merchandise without arousing the suspicion of the authorities or the suppliers.

Fences fall into various categories. At the bottom of this hierarchy is the local fence who serves the neighborhood. A local fence can operate out of a garage, bar, or restaurant. Many local fences function as conduits for the distribution of goods acquired in scam operations.

There are various other categories of fences, however, but the key to a successful scam operation is a large outlet fence.[12] Such a fence consists of a business that handles legitimate merchandise but also handles large volumes of low-cost goods that may be either stolen or the product of a bankruptcy fraud. The outlet fence can purchase large volumes of merchandise and thus provide a market for the scam operators. This business fence may operate through a series of middlemen, and its management may not even be aware that the goods are the product of an illicit operation.[13] Suffice it to say, however, that without this large outlet, scam operators would find it more difficult to evade detection and prosecution. Bankruptcy fraud is a big business; it undermines our confidence in the financial institutions of this country, as well as in our system of credit. Thousands of small and large businesses are victimized yearly. Needless to say, the cost is ultimately borne by the consuming public. In large part, scams are facilitated by our present bankruptcy laws and by the failure of our prosecutorial machinery to react with the requisite effectiveness. The laws make it easy to evade prosecution through the veil of bankruptcy, and the onus is placed on the individual to investigate and uncover these frauds. Undeniably, our bankruptcy laws play an important role. However, they must be brought into line with the needs of our present society. There is a pressing need for reassessment and action in this area.

Notes

1. Report by the New York State Commission of Investigation, *Racketeer Infiltration into Legitimate Business* (New York: New York State Commission on Investigation, 1970), pp. 49-50.

2. Chamber of Commerce of the United States, *White Collar Crime* (Washington, D.C.: Chamber of Commerce of the United States, 1974), p.

13; for additional background information, see also, Chamber of Commerce of the United States, *Marshaling Citizen Power Against Crime* (Washington, D.C.: Chamber of Commerce of the United States, 1970), pp. 1-10.

3. Chamber of Commerce of the United States, *White Collar Crime*, pp. 6, 13.

4. U.S. Const., Art. 1, sec. 8, par. 4.

5. *United States* v. *Castellana*, 349 F.2d 264 (2d Cir. 1965), cert. denied 383 U.S. 928; see also, 11 U.S.C.A., sec. 22(b).

6. 11 U.S.C.A., secs. 104, 107(c).

7. See Comment, "Bankruptcy: The Strong-Arm Claus," 5 *Vill. L, Rev.* 437 (1960).

8. 11 U.S.C.A., sec. 21; see also, Note, "Acts of Bankruptcy in Perspective," 67 *Harv. L. Rev.* 500 (1954).

9. *United States* v. *Castellana*, 349 F.2d 264 (2d Cir. 1965), cert. denied 383 U.S. 928.

10. Report by the New York State Commission of Investigation, *Racketeer Infiltration Into Legitimate Business*, pp. 89, 90.

11. G. Robert Blakey and Michael Goldsmith, "Criminal Redistribution of Stolen Property: The Need for Law Reform," *Mich. L. Rev.* 74 (August 1976):1523.

12. Ibid., p. 1531.

13. Ibid.

6

Bribes, Kickbacks, and Political Frauds

Recently, a city employee in Ann Arbor, Michigan, was dismissed for speculating with more than $100 million of city funds.[1] In New York, a state investigation disclosed that more than 200 judges may have been involved in a massive scheme to "fix" traffic tickets in exchange for political favors.[2] Not to be outdone, a large New York based company disclosed that over a period of several years it had paid more than $4 million in bribes to induce businessmen to purchase its products.[3]

The extent of bribery, kickbacks, and political frauds exceeds billions of dollars annually. Some sources put the figure at more than $3 billion.[4] This undermines any confidence the public may have in both the business and political sectors of our society. The problem is so serious that in some cities businessmen cannot operate without paying large bribes to local politicians. In one large New Jersey city, both the mayor and several city councilmen had to be paid $10,000 each in bribes in order for a company to obtain a contract with the city.[5] The problem is so pervasive that one New York union has threatened to call for a strike by its membership unless steps are taken to put a stop to the practice.[6] The union officials were concerned because their members were being used to funnel bribes and kickbacks. The situation merits serious concern.

Understanding the Problem

In 1966 the mayor of New York City appointed a new commissioner for water, gas, and electricity. Unfortunately for the city, the new commissioner had many debts. To meet his obligations, he turned to friends, since the job paid only $30,000 a year. When the city's reservoirs needed draining and cleaning, an opportunity presented itself. The work was actually worth about $500,000, but the commissioner authorized that more than $800,000 be paid.[7] In return, the contractor secretly agreed to pay 2 percent of the total value of the contract to the commissioner—this was the kickback.

Kickbacks, bribes, and political corruption usually go hand-in-hand. They are not new, nor are they characteristic only of our society. Their objectives are usually to gain some competitive edge, to obtain or retain business or services, or to cover up inferior products or short deliveries. They may involve two or more companies dealing with one another, or the

41

private sector and the bureaucracy, or the elected elements at either the local or federal level. The law enforcement apparatus—judges, policemen, and even prosecutors—are also usually involved at some level within any scheme.

These frauds have indicators. For example, in some localities the same firms are consistently awarded contracts for services or products, while more qualified firms are refused entry into the government contract market. Politicians, bureaucrats, and members of the judiciary are usually seen accompanying individuals from these firms, or they are seen in the company of individuals known to have criminal records.[8] City costs seem to increase constantly, while other localities seem to be paying less for more.[9] Bureaucrats and politicians, once they leave service, seem to join firms connected with those who have city or state contracts. Law firms connected with political figures consistently represent corporations that have won government contracts. The police are not enforcing the laws.[10] Prosecutors do not seem to be bringing the accused before the courts. To the average citizen, something is not well in "Denmark." These are the symptoms of bribery, kickbacks, and political frauds.

Private Corruption

We tend to associate corruption with government officials. However, bribery and kickbacks are also found in the private sector. Private corruption may involve payments from one firm to another, or payments from the firm itself, to officers and directors of that firm. For example, one large beer company was accused by federal investigators of making more than $3 million in illegal payments to numerous other firms in order to induce them to use its beer.[11] The payments were in violation of both state and federal liquor licensing laws. The company employed numerous techniques, including such shams as payments for advertising and phony contracts. Further, to conceal the illegal payments, the firm falsified its books and records, hiding the activity from both federal agencies and its own stockholders.

A large restaurant chain disclosed that it had received more than $500,000 over a period of several years in payoffs from suppliers. The money was an inducement for the restaurant to purchase meats, milk, and other products from these suppliers rather than from their competitors.[12] One of the chain's subsidiaries had itself paid $16,000 to an airline official to get that firm's business.[13] In large urban centers like New York, one out of every seven dollars exchanging hands may be tainted with commercial bribery.[14] In large part, this results from the fact that most states have no commercial bribery statutes. Those that do (less than a dozen) make it a misdemeanor, usually punishable by a small fine and/or a small prison sentence. However, few if any individuals are indicted for commercial bribery, and fewer still ever go to prison.[15]

Private corruption also involves the firm itself—for example, payments in the form of loans and services to officers and directors of the company. One large firm, with annual sales of over $50 million, paid annual salaries of more than $100,000 to family members who rendered no work or services to the company.[16] In addition, the firm also paid the rental and maintenance fees for apartments occupied by family members of officers and directors of the company, as well as the college tuitions for relatives. In a related case, a Boston waste removal firm was charged by federal prosecutors with funneling more than $3 million in company money for the personal use of its officers and directors.[17] One of the firm's officers sold land to the company at an inflated price of over $2 million. An executive with one of the nation's largest banks took more than $500,000 in kickbacks from a brokerage house on the West Coast in exchange for his promise to buy and sell stock through that firm.[18] One transaction alone resulted in losses of more than $3 million to clients of the bank. In another case, a large national firm paid the salaries for the servants of one of its directors.[19] The firm also forgave more than $1 million owed to it by one of its officers, and it paid the expenses for the upkeep of a director's yacht.

Commercial bribery involving American firms also occurs overseas. Payments have been made to numerous foreign corporations and to foreign subsidiaries of American firms. During the 1960s, several American firms made payments to South Vietnamese and Thai firms to induce them to purchase their products and services.[20] The illegal payments were not disclosed to stockholders back in this country, nor to federal agencies charged with policing the economy. In many instances, the payments were kept secret from foreign governments as well.

Bureaucratic Bribery

With the turn of the century, the reformist movements produced a civil service system in both the federal and state bureaucracies. The civil service system has given rise to new forms of bribery—bureaucratic corruption.[21] The former assistant director of the school system of a large Pennsylvania city received monthly payoffs from a school food contracting firm.[22] In Baltimore, Maryland, prosecutors uncovered a scheme to sell exam answers to civil service system applicants.[23] In Brooklyn, New York, a state highway inspector was indicted along with several business associates and charged with receiving bribes.[24]

Corruption by bureaucrats is by no means limited to the state level. At

the federal level, the Federal Housing Administration (FHA) has been involved in a number of scandals. Several years ago, more than 300 individuals were indicted as an outgrowth of an intensive federal investigation. FHA frauds involved the purchase of inner-city housing and bribes
paid by contractors to FHA agents to inflate the value of the property.[25]
Speculators made large profits.

The Small Business Administration (SBA) has also been racked by
fraud.[26] Charges of corruption and allegations of payoffs have been
directed at many SBA officers.[27] SBA loans have been made to political
associates of high government officials, and many of these ventures have
gone into bankruptcy. As always, the bill was paid by the public. SBA
bureaucrats, under political pressure, usually acquiesce.

The rise of the civil service system has not materially affected the corrupt practices of the old days. It has served to refine and change their form,
though, and kickbacks and bribes have taken on a new dimension. Instead
of paying the bureaucrat (although this still occurs in many instances), a
lucrative position is promised him when he leaves government. Political
support for advancement within the bureaucracy is a frequent alternative.
In some instances, the bribe takes the appearance of an investment. For example, California state revenue agents sold stock in a company they owned
to individuals who had problems with the state taxing agency.[28] Bribery has
taken on new dimensions, and the bureaucrat has joined ranks with the
politician.

Political Bribery

Corruption involving political figures takes on two forms: (1) domestic,
and (2) foreign. Domestic political corruption goes back to the nineteenth
century. However, with the growth of cities, local political corruption increased.[29] Recent revelations have shown that political corruption is neither
limited nor inconsequential.[30] The mayor of a large Indiana city reported
that a $100,000 bribe offer had been made to him; and a candidate for the
office of attorney general in a New England state was also offered a bribe of
similar size.[31] A survey of 59 business executives found that 29 of these had
been asked to make domestic payments to increase their respective firms'
sales.[32] The survey found that domestic requests for political payments were
greater than those abroad. One large tire manufacturer paid more than
$200,000 to state and local political figures in a four-year period.[33] Another
large tire manufacturer paid over $300,000 in domestic political payoffs
during a three-year period.[34]

Political bribery is ingrained in the fiber of many of our local governments. A National Crime Commission study of one Pennsylvania

city—Wincanton (a fictitious name given the city to disguise it)—found that its political fiber was so controlled by political bribery and kickbacks that one could not conduct business within its boundaries without making payments to some officials and even the mayor himself.[35] Other cities, like Chicago, Illinois, and Newark, New Jersey, have been in the clutches of organized criminal elements for many years.[36] In Newark the mayor and several of his associates bilked contractors of more than $1 million in kickbacks.[37]

One of the more startling stories involving political bribery and kickbacks involved Vice President Spiro T. Agnew. In 1962 he ran for the office of Baltimore County Executive. Later he ran successfully for the office of governor of Maryland. Once in the governor's mansion, Mr. Agnew embarked on a scheme—long practiced in that state—of asking for kickbacks from contractors who did business with the state.[38] Firms that made payments to the governor's agents stood an excellent chance of obtaining the state contracts.[39] One company alone paid over $10,000 in fees each year while Mr. Agnew was governor.[40]

Political corruption is not limited to the domestic arena. Bribery and kickbacks to foreign government officials have been common, and there is every reason to believe that they will continue.[41] A large aerospace corporation was charged with making questionable payments of almost $38 million to foreign government officials.[42] More than $12 million was paid to Japanese government officials, with more than $1 million possibly being paid to a former prime minister of that country. Another large aerospace firm has been charged with making over $30 million in questionable payments to numerous foreign officials and agents.[43] Payments are usually made to agents, or deposited in secret bank accounts; sometimes they are paid under the guise of consulting fees. Payments have also gone to political parties, to leftist guerilla groups operating in Latin America and the Middle East, and even to politicians in Communist countries.[44] These payments have not only undermined this country's standing abroad, but also that of political figures who have sided with the West. Political corruption can have, and has had, devastating effects on the domestic social fiber of this nation.

Electioneering Frauds

A democracy's survival rests on the legitimate support of its citizens. When the latter begin to view it with cynicism and regard it as illegitimate, then the days of that democracy are numbered. Since the free electioneering process forms the very basis of a democracy, tampering with that process can ultimately have damaging effects. Electioneering frauds can arise from one of two sources: (1) domestic groups, and (2) foreign agents. Historically, domestic groups have manipulated and tampered with the election process (especially at the local level). However, with the advent of the Cold War, as the United States began to assume a global role, the outcome of domestic elections became the concern also of outside political interests. Although not fully studied and documented, save for the South Korean scandal, there can be little doubt that foreign interests have attempted, and have possibly affected, the electioneering process in this country.

Electioneering frauds have as their objective the denial of the democratic process; they seek to manipulate the election and bring about the victory of their side. This is accomplished by one of two ways: (1) the role of party workers, and (2) the assistance of election officials. Party workers play a key role in any election. They can register unqualified voters, either under fictitious names or by falsifying records. They can also assist in stuffing ballot boxes. Election officials can be intimidated, as can non-friendly voters. In addition, large numbers of opposition ballots can be destroyed. The party worker is the infantry. He can also be employed (as has been the case in many cities) to fight off opposing party workers and to intimidate local businessmen into making contributions.

Election officials, friendly to the party, can be employed to falsify electoral records and to pad registration books. Tally sheets can also be altered and fabricated; election officials themselves may be directly involved in these frauds. These officials may also be involved in the destruction of absentee-voter ballots, further supporting "their" party. In cases involving automated election machines, these can be tampered with and, where necessary, sabotaged. Election officials are usually selected for their loyalty to the group in power and can play a key role in assisting in an electioneering fraud. To ensure that neither they nor the party workers are prosecuted, the local political machinery will put pressure on friendly or party prosecutors and judges to quash any attempts to bring about a successful prosecution of those involved in the fraud.

Elections can also be affected by foreign interference. News has surfaced of South Korean attempts to influence the votes of U.S. Congressmen.[45] However, it would be a simple process for foreign agents to support, through funds and other forms of assistance, candidates they found appealing. The United States has done this abroad, and there is little reason to doubt that it can be reciprocated.[46] During the seventeenth century, European powers interfered in the election of Polish legislators. They supported those who served their interests best. In an electronic society, it would be a simple mattter for foreign agents to blackmail or expose the weaknesses and sexual tastes of opposing political candidates, ensuring victory for their candidate. It would be naive indeed to think that this either has not occurred, or that we are immune from such interference.

Various theories have been offered to explain commercial and political corruption in American society. It is said that we attach great value to private gain and that we lack the ability to resist temptations. In great part, this is true. However, the same can be said of any society. It is also said that our system of division of powers creates a state of checks, and that political and commercial corruption tend to break this deadlock. To this one can add only that a society that does so, seriously tampers with its freedoms. We need only look at the great nations and peoples of the past.

Bribery, kickbacks, and political frauds have been with us for many years. They have taken their toll—Watergate alone fully illustrates this tragedy. We have paid in terms of higher prices, poorer services, and an erosion of our system of governance. Hopefully, we can learn from the tragedies of other great nations—the pursuit of corruption led to their demise.

Notes

1. "City Fund Speculation," *Washington Post*, October 7, 1977, p. A-9.

2. "Ticket Fixing by Judges," *Washington Post*, June 21, 1977, p. A-16.

3. "National Distillers Says that Liquor Unit Paid Kickbacks of $4 Million to Retailers," *Wall Street Journal*, January 1, 1977, p. 5.

4. Chamber of Commerce of the United States, *White Collar Crime* (Washington, D.C.: Chamber of Commerce of the United States, 1974), p. 6; see also, Chamber of Commerce of the United States, *Deskbook on Organized Crime* (Washington, D.C.: Chamber of Commerce of the United States, 1972).

5. Michael Dorman, *Payoff: The Role of Organized Crime in American Politics* (New York: David McKay, 1972), pp. 54-60.

6. Jonathan Kwitny, "Liquor Salesmen Vow to Cease Role in Kickback Racket," *Wall Street Journal*, December 1, 1976, p. 1.

7. Michael Dorman, *Payoff: The Role of Organized Crime in American Politics*, pp. 78-90.

8. Nicholas Gage, "Organized Crime in Court," in *Theft of the City*, John A. Gardiner and David J. Olson, eds. (Bloomington, Indiana: Indiana Univ. Press, 1974), p. 165.

9. John A. Gardiner and David J. Olson, eds., *Theft of the City*, p. 239.

10. John A. Gardiner, "The Stern Syndicate in Wincanton," in *Theft of the City*, pp. 97-99.

11. "SEC Accuses Schlitz Brewing of Making at Least $3 Million in Illegal Payments," *Wall Street Journal*, April 8, 1977, p. 5.

12. "Restaurant Firm Discloses Payoffs by its Suppliers," *Wall Street Journal*, March 23, 1977, p. 16.

13. Ibid.

14. Interview by myself with prosecutors involved in commercial bribery cases.

15. Most of the commercial bribery cases, once brought to prosecution, have culminated in consent degrees. These are agreements whereby the defendant neither denies nor admits his guilt, but agrees not to commit any further violations.

16. John F. Berry, "SEC Says Liquor Firm Made Illegal Payments," *Washington Post*, October 18, 1977, p. D-11.

17. Bradley Graham, "SEC Sues IN Payoffs, Theft Ring," *Washington Post*, August 9, 1977, pp. D-7, D-11.

18. John F. Berry, "Kickbacks Laid to Bankers Trust Official," *Washington Post*, December 22, 1976, p. E-8.

19. Timothy D. Schellhardt, "Those Business Payoffs Didn't All Go Abroad; Bosses Got Some Too," *Wall Street Journal*, May 2, 1977, p. 1.

20. Based on my experience while employed at the Securities and Exchange Commission.

21. Arnold J. Heidenheimer, "Definitions, Concepts and Criteria," in *Theft of the City*, p. 19.

22. "Philadelphia D.A. Obtains Perjury Conviction from Kick-back Investigation," *National District Attorneys Association Economic Crime Digest* (March and April 1976): 117.

23. "Firemen Grease Promotional Ladder," *National District Attorneys Association Economic Crime Digest* (June-July 1975):108.

24. "Housing Frauds," *National District Attorneys Association Economic Crime Digest* (October-November 1974):290.

25. Public Citizens Staff Report, *White Collar Crime* (Washington, D.C.: Congress Watch, 1974), pp. 22, 23.

26. Ibid., pp. 23, 24.

27. Based on my interviews with several federal prosecutors.

28. Kefauver Committee, "Official Corruption and Organized Crime," in *Theft of the City*, p. 69.

29. John A. Gardiner and David J. Olson, *Theft of the City*, p. 4.

30. See Donald R. Cressey, *Theft of the Nation* (New York: Harper & Row, 1969), pp. 248-290, for a review of corruption in government.

31. Ralph Salerno and John S. Tompkins, "Protecting Organized Crime," in *Theft of the City*, p. 146.

32. "A Whiff of Bribery on the Home Front," *New York Times*, May 16, 1976, p. F-15.

33. John F. Berry, "Retain General Tire President, Panel on Payments Says," *Washington Post*, July 20, 1977, p. D-8.

34. John F. Berry, "Former Firestone Tire Official Headed Secret Fund, SEC Told," *Washington Post*, December 24, 1976, p. C-5.

35. John A. Gardiner, "The Stern Syndicate in Wincanton," in *Theft of the City*, p. 97.

36. Mike Royko, *Boss: Richard J. Daley* (New York: E.P. Dutton, 1971), pp. 59-65.

37. Ron Porambo, "An Autopsy of Newark," in *Theft of the City*, p. 87.

38. George Beall, "Kickbacks on Engineering Contracts in Maryland," in *Theft of the City*, pp. 258, 261.

39. Ibid., p. 265.

40. Ibid., p. 270.

41. Based on my interviews with law enforcement sources.

42. William H. Jones and John F. Berry, "Lockheed Paid $38 Million in Bribes Abroad," *Washington Post*, May 27, 1977, p. E-9.

43. "A Question of Bribery," *Newsweek*, April 18, 1975, p. 70.

44. John F. Berry, "Retain General Tire President, Panel on Payments Says," p. D-8.

45. T.R. Reid, "Hanna Indicted in Korean Bribery Case," *Washington Post*, October 15, 1977, p. A-10.

46. John F. Berry, "Retain General Tire President, Panel on Payments Says," p. D-8.

7 Consumer-Related Frauds

The prosecutor for a large Midwestern city charged several stores with violating the state's false advertising and unfair trade practices statutes.[1] In Florida, state prosecutors charged that more than 70,000 people from over 30 states may have lost up to $1 billion in real estate fraud schemes.[2] In Pennsylvania, the president of a driving school was charged with more than 20 counts of mail fraud and one count of conspiracy.[3] Over a period of several years in more than a dozen states, the defendant had advertised driving lessons with a guarantee of a job after graduation. Consumers paid up to $1000 each for a three-week course.

Consumer fraud is a serious problem that is, unfortunately, on the increase. Some sources put losses at more than $20 billion annually.[4] Federal authorities estimate that auto repair frauds alone account for more than $10 billion lost by consumers each year.[5] More than 800 categories of consumer frauds have been identified to date.[6] They include everything from charity frauds to free medical clinics that eventually bilk the consumer through expensive and unnecessary treatments to home repair frauds. As the number of frauds increase, so do the victims, which include businesses as well as individuals. The outcome is a nationwide loss of confidence in both our political and economic systems. Consumer fraud covers all forms of financial transactions and assumes various forms. It is, perhaps in some ways, the most insidious form of fraud, for it is aimed at the naive and unsuspecting members of our society.

Defining Consumer Fraud

Consumer *fraud* may be defined as an intentional act to cause another to surrender money or property over which he has a right. It is a false or misleading representation of a material fact, whether by words or conduct, that causes a consumer to be deceived. At times, it may take the form of the concealment of a material fact. The objective of consumer fraud is to deceive the consumer into acting to his legal detriment. Consumer frauds are essentially confidence games, usually contrived to appeal to the greed of the victim.[7]

Almost all our local jurisdictions, as well as the federal government, have enacted some sort of provisions to deal with these frauds. At the federal level, the mail fraud statutes provide for penalties and fines for frauds and swindles that make use of the U.S. Postal Service.[8] The federal fraud-by-wire statute makes it a felony, punishable by both imprisonment and/or a fine, to cause to be transmitted by means of a wire, radio, or television any writings, sounds, or pictures for the purpose of defrauding the public.[9]

At the local level, the era of mass advertising signaled the end of many of the common-law remedies for victims of consumer fraud. The buyer-seller situation took on new dimensions. Early warranty law and actions in fraud and deceit proved too narrow and confining to allow the consumer any remedy. Many states passed numerous statutes to address this problem. Some localities provided not only civil but also criminal sanctions for consumer fraud acts.

Although state laws concentrate on various general categories of consumer fraud, prosecutions at the local level revolve around one or more of the following six theories: (1) conspiracy, (2) perjury, (3) false representation, (4) theft by trick, (5) false pretenses, and (6) forgery. Any one or more of these theories of law may be applied in the area of consumer fraud.

A *conspiracy* is usually defined as a combination for an unlawful purpose. It is one of the oldest and most successful prosecutorial tools. The gist of the crime of conspiracy is the combination of two or more individuals to accomplish a criminal objective. A lone individual cannot be said to be involved in a conspiracy. There must also be a unity of mind and design. No formal agreement need be shown by the prosecutors. The understanding can be inferred from the circumstances surrounding the case, but there must be a meeting of the minds of the parties involved. Under the common law, no overt act was necessary, and some state statutes have actually included this requirement in their conspiracy laws. The conspiracy itself does not merge with the end objective—the illegal act. It is a powerful tool, and one that can serve well in the consumer fraud area.

Many states have perjury laws, thereby addressing the second prosecutorial theory. Under the common law, *perjury* was limited to judicial proceedings. Statutes now include many nonjudicial matters; and in many jurisdictions it is a felony to make a willful and corrupt statement, either in writing or orally, as regards a material matter. The perjury may take the form of a false affidavit, false testimony before an investigative or legislative body, or false testimony in a trial. At both the federal and local level, various officers have been designated, by statute, the power to administer oaths. False testimony after such an oath is administered can result in perjury charges. For example, the Internal Revenue Service (as well as the other federal investigatory bodies) referred a number of such cases to the Justice Department for prosecution.

A *false representation* has been defined as a statement made willfully, to deceive another, that is not true. It may take the form of a false promise or a concealment of the truth. A *theft by trick* is usually a misrepresentation of past or present fact, with the intent to defraud the consumer—the perpetrator must have knowledge of the falsity of his representations. Further, the victim must rely on these particular falsities and surrender either his money and/or property. Although the victim relinquishes possession, he does not surrender title to the property and/or money. Most consumer frauds can be prosecuted under these statutes.

The charge of *false pretenses* involves an intent to defraud a consumer through misrepresentations of past or present material facts. The victim must rely on these falsities and must surrender his property and/or money to the criminal because of this reliance. The intent of the victim must be to surrender not only possession but also title. The felon must have knowledge of the falsity.

Many categories of consumer fraud usually involve some form of forgery. Generally, *forgery* is the making of a false writing that has some apparent legal significance. There are three key elements to this offense: (1) the writing itself must be the possible subject of forgery, (2) the writing must be false, and (3) the writing must be made with the intent to defraud the victim. Under common law, forgery was a misdemeanor, but presently many state statutes make it a felony. However, it is not sufficient for the document to declare a falsity, it must actually be a false document. The forgery may be committed by one who uses fictitious names or obtains the signature of another for a fraudulent objective.

Many states, and a number of courts, have provided consumers with the right to bring private actions against the perpetrators of frauds. Arizona courts have interpreted that state's Consumer Fraud Act and Fraudulent Advertising Practices Act as allowing the consumer such a right of action.[10] In the case of *Rice* v. *Snarlin*, an Illinois court recognized the right of consumers to bring private action under that state's consumer statute.[11] Oregon allows consumers to bring private actions under its consumer act for any losses suffered through the fraudulent act of the seller.[12]

Prosecuting consumer fraud cases, as with other white-collar crimes, is seriously hampered by various drawbacks. It is difficult, for example, to prove that, in fact, the outcome was the product of a willful intent to defraud the public rather than an error in business judgement. In addition, the felons in these cases argue that their agents, and not they, were behind the scheme. Proving that both agent and principal acted jointly is rarely an easy task. Felons also argue, in defense, that it is merely salesmanship, that in every business there concededly is an element of "puffing." Liability is difficult to attach to the actual manipulators, and as a consequence, prosecution usually takes the form of an injunction or consent agreement. Criminal actions are rare and hampered by a judiciary that metes out lenient sentences against those convicted of these frauds.

Categories of Consumer Fraud

Frauds against consumers may involve crimes by an individual against another individual or a business, or crimes by a business against an individual or another business. These frauds take on numerous forms and shades. They may involve one or more felons and can range from simple swindles to complex and international frauds. They encompass real estate, the medical and health arena, merchandise, advertising, charity and religion, travel, schools and training, home improvement schemes, and many more. This section will cover the frauds that are more prevalent and of greater concern to the public and prosecutors.

One of the more common and pervasive forms of consumer fraud involves the home improvement area. In a New York case, more than 10 people were indicted on more than 200 counts of forgery, fraud, and grand larceny in an elaborate home improvement fraud that bilked home owners of more than $100,000 in one year alone.[13] Without the knowledge of the owners, the defendants had obtained mortgages on the properties in excess of the amount involved in the improvement. Home owners had also been told that they would receive good repairs at low prices. In Vermont, local prosecutors charged a New Hampshire firm with defrauding state home owners.[14] The victims had unknowingly signed mortgages on their homes. In Colorado, federal investigators charged two home improvement firms with falsely representing that their home improvements would reduce fuel bills by 50 percent, and that their home siding was guaranteed by a major U.S. steel maker.[15] The victims were also told that this offer would only be available for a limited period of time.

The preceding are examples of home improvement frauds. The perpetrators usually promise the home owner low-cost renovation of his home. In return, they may require substantial down payments. There is no real intent to complete the work; and since many times the owner is not given a completion date, prosecution can be very difficult. Guarantees on workmanship are rarely put in writing; they are usually oral and vague. When the work falls in arrears or is shabby, the perpetrators usually declare bankruptcy or leave the jurisdiction. Many times the work is never completed at all. Occasionally, the home owner is offered a loan, which appears legitimate at first sight. The promoters may then sell the owner's note, at a discount, to a finance company, without the owner's consent or knowledge. The finance company, under the guise of a holder in due course, collects the monthly payments on the loan.

If the promoter fails to perform the contracted repairs, the home owner must continue to pay his monthly payments to the finance company. The law is explicit on this point. As a holder in due course, the finance company took the note after paying for it; it did so in good faith—unless the aggrieved consumer can show otherwise. This is extremely difficult to prove. The consumer must show that the finance company knew or should have known that this was a fraud, and that the finance company knew or should have known the home repair agreement was a sham. Proof is again difficult, and it may very well be that the finance company actually had no knowledge of the sham. Whatever the case, the consumer is the loser. The finance company is entitled to the monthly payments, and the promoter has been paid for the note. Although the home owner did not know that the finance company purchased the note, he has no defense.

Energy-related frauds are also common and, with the advent of the energy crisis, can be expected to increase dramatically. These schemes take advantage of the public's naivete in technical matters. The promoters promise that their devices will save fuel and money for the consumer. One mail order firm sold a device called "Unitron" that was said to save fuel, when in fact it was found to be worthless.[16] In a California case, the manufacturer of a gas-saving device promised consumers that his invention would save them as much as 50 percent on their gasoline bill, and that it would also reduce auto pollution by as much as 70 percent.[17] Government tests showed no significant gas savings through use of this device. The manufacturer was fined $26,000 and agreed to cease making any further such claims. However, the public had already lost more than $200,000 in 12 months. Energy-related frauds may have cost the public more than $100 million in one year alone.[18]

An equally serious problem is that of deceptive advertising. With the growth of mass media, false and misleading advertising has taken on a national dimension and continues to be a serious and growing problem. The consuming public is barraged with false and misleading information regarding a product or service. It is told that this quality product is available for a limited time only at a very low price. The objective of the deception is to induce the naive public to come to the store. Once there, an individual may be told that the advertised product has been sold out, but an equally good substitute is available. A salesman may tell him that for a "few more dollars" he can buy a much better product, and that in fact the advertised product is a "cheap" one. At times, the advertised product may have been purposely tampered with to give it a cheaper appearance.

Once the consumer is baited (through the deceptive advertising) and enters the store, the promoters can then control the environment and induce him to buy the product they originally intended to sell. The advertisement was only the bait. These practices are commonly referred to as *bait-and-switch advertising*. They have proven amazingly successful. For example, one Minnesota firm baited consumers with false advertisements of $120 worth of meals for the price of $7.95.[19] In another case, a firm offered to repair an auto transmission for $69.50; and then, once the car was on the lift, raised its prices substantially.[20] A drug store chain misled the public by offering phony sales on its products.[21] The sale price was really the regular selling price of the product; there was, in fact, no sale. Unfortunately, frauds are not limited to sellers of products alone. They also encompass sellers of services. For example, health spas have been found selling memberships in nonexistent facilities.[22] Further, the promoters have employed high-pressure sales tactics and have offered phony bargains.

Under pressure from consumers, many states have passed legislation prohibiting false and misleading advertising. Some statutes include representations of any form, whether oral or written.[23] Several states provide not only civil penalties but also criminal sanctions.[24] Other states have more specific statutes, which deal with such areas as the advertisement of phony sales and other bait-and-switch tactics.[25] At the federal level, the Federal Trade Commission Act makes it illegal to use false and misleading advertisements in the area of foods, drugs, and cosmetics.[26] One of the better known federal cases involved a national firm that advertised that its shaving cream made it possible to shave even sandpaper.[27] What the advertisement did not tell the public was that the sandpaper was really glass with sand sprayed on its surface.

Through statutes, many states allow consumers to bring their own private litigation and also provide for recovery of attorney's fees if victorious.[28] Since consumer-related litigation can be long and expensive (especially where large firms are involved as defendants), the state had hoped to provide the consumer with an added leverage. The successes, however, have proven limited and short term. Few attorneys are willing to accept a case on the contingency of receiving fees, if victorious, somewhere down the road. Few consumers can afford the initial costs of litigation. For example, depositions and travel costs, especially where witnesses may be spread nationally, can be expensive, and few attorneys are willing to spend their own funds based on the possibility of being compensated only if victorious. Further, the defendants themselves have not taken this lying down. Some of these statutes have been attacked as unconstitutional on the grounds of being vague.[29] In addition, most statutes provide only for civil remedies. Although the noncriminal elements may be deterred, the real criminal will not.

Land fraud schemes have cost the consumer billions of dollars in the last several years. In one case, a large Miami-based firm offered for sale lots in Florida and Arizona. It represented them as being an excellent opportunity to invest in real estate at almost no risk to the consumer.[30] Dinner parties and high-pressure selling tactics were employed. The public was not told that the lots were undeveloped, and that the firm did not plan to build any sewage or water systems. In another case, more than 20,000 consumers were bilked out of more than $200 million through a series of real estate fraud schemes.[31] In one nationwide fraud, over 40,000 individuals were sold some

70,000 lots of desert land in New Mexico for as much as $10,000 per acre.[32] The buyers were told that the land would soon be developed, and that it represented a risk-free investment. The promoters were later charged by a federal grand jury with 70 counts of mail fraud. Several hundred million dollars of investors' money was involved.

Land fraud swindles often use the lure of vacation and retirement property to dupe their victims. Worthless real estate, such as desert or swamp land, is usually sold for high prices. Picturesque brochures and even films are employed to win consumer interest. The victim is told that "land is the best investment" in the world, that he cannot go wrong with the land. Resale values are exaggerated. Promises of future improvements are made, and these usually are either never begun or never completed. Deeds and other key documents are rarely delivered. When the buyer finally visits his "dreamland," he may find that there are no streets, golf courses, or other recreational parks in the vicinity.

Some states have acted to cut down on frauds in this area. For example, California requires that a developer inform buyers of provisions taken for water, utilities, sewer, fill, and soil conditions.[33] At the federal level, the Inter-state Land Sales Act also requires a developer to furnish a buyer with a report on the land involved, provided the buyer has not seen the land himself at first sight.[34] The act also provides for civil and criminal penalties. Courts have held sellers of real estate liable where a buyer has suffered damages;[35] but unless malice or fraud is shown, courts have been reluctant to apply punitive damages.[36] Consequently, the problem continues. Criminal prosecutions have been infrequent and inconclusive. Even when convicted, the swindler is assured a lenient sentence—usually probation and a small fine. The majority of these frauds are prosecuted civilly by such agencies as the Federal Trade Commission and state attorney general offices. These prosecutions often culminate in consent decrees and small fines, thus leaving the injured buyer to fend for himself.

Several years ago, two con men established an organization by the name of HELP.[37] They then hired the services of some students and launched a major charity drive. The unsuspecting public was told that the funds collected by HELP would be used to aid underprivileged children. The unsuspecting public was taken for thousands of dollars before the fraud was uncovered. In another charity fraud, several con men launched a similar drive; they represented to the unsuspecting public that the proceeds from the sales of some of their products would be used to help the handicapped.[38] As it turned out, the handicapped never saw the proceeds. Members of the group were later prosecuted for mail fraud violations.

Charity frauds take on many forms. In general, the promoters represent to the unsuspecting consumer that his funds will be used to assist the needy and underprivileged or will be given to some deserving organization. The beneficiaries of this drive are described only in general terms; the consumer is not told what percentage of the proceeds will go to the needy. The firm behind the drive is usually a shell for the promoters, with no history in the area of charity work.[39] It may, on occasion, adopt the name of a well-known group. For example, one well-organized con operation impersonated police officers and solicited donations under the guise that these proceeds would be used to help a police union.[40] Contributors were told that in return for their kindness, they would receive greater police protection. Some of the con men even flashed badges. Where necessary, high-pressure tactics were employed. The public was bilked heavily.

Not surprisingly, auto-related frauds run into the billions. These schemes range from phony devices that purportedly save gasoline to auto rebates. Many of these frauds deal with misrepresentations in terms of the needs for, and extent of, repairs. In some instances, no repairs are made at all. In a case from Westchester County, New York, more than 35 firms were suspected of having bilked the public of millions of dollars through auto-related frauds.[42] The offenses ranged from mileage rollbacks to the falsification of repair records.

With the large increase in applications to professional schools (especially medical and dental schools), a new form of consumer fraud has begun to attract the attention of con men—the education- or school-related swindles. One such con man took unsuspecting students for more than $1 million by promising to place them in professional schools.[43] The victims paid him fees ranging from $5000 to $25,000. In another scheme, a correspondence school offered courses in livestock buying and promised its victims that lucrative and rewarding jobs would await them.[44] The courses were worthless, and there were no jobs for the victims. These frauds are directed at the young and the discontented, who are lured by promises of an exciting and rewarding career. False representations are made as to the value of the courses and possibilities for employment.[45] In many cases, the fraud is directed specifically toward veterans and minority groups.

As the public begins to have more time for leisure and more funds for vacations, new frauds come into being. One of the newest and fastest growing is that related to travel. The swindle may take many forms. For example, one such fraud directed its focus on the terminally ill, who were promised "psychic surgery" tours to foreign lands.[46] Another such scheme involved "quickie divorces" in the Caribbean. The victims were told that by purchasing a package tour, they would also be able to obtain legal divorces in a matter of days rather than months or even years back in the United States.[47]

One of the fastest and most successful of all consumer-related frauds is that of idea promotion. Each year, inventors pay various firms more than $100 million to patent and promote their inventions.[48] Much of this money goes into the pockets of fraud artists. These promoters promise the inventors contact with manufacturers, both here and abroad, who may be interested in their inventions. In return, they ask for a share of the royalties and an initial fee of about $1000. In reality, these firms do little for the inventor, and the meager service actually rendered in hardly worth the large fee the inventor pays. One such swindle covered 18 states and took numerous inventors for large sums of money.[49] Individuals paid fees of as much as $1800. In fact, the promoters did little to market their inventions. The problem with these swindles is that they are difficult to prove as frauds. These con men never fully spell out exactly what they will do for the inventor. Thus it is very difficult to prove a fraud, since they can always show that they have, in fact, performed some work. The fact that the work was worthless is insufficient to support a charge of fraud.

Business opportunity swindles are perhaps the oldest and one of the most serious of the consumer-related frauds. They vary in form but not substance. The objective is to induce the consumer to invest his money in the scheme by misrepresenting the real worth of the business. Specific promises are never reduced to a written agreement, nor are references given. The consumer is promised large profits for little, if any, work. One of the more common of these swindles is the "work-at-home" scheme. Experts estimate that this scheme alone bilks consumers of over $500 million annually.[50] This type of fraud usually preys on the old, the retired, and the average housewife. It takes advantage of their need for extra income. The victim is promised large profits for little or no effort. For a small sum of money, the victim can invest in this business venture; no experience is necessary. There are promises of assistance from the promoter.

These swindles take a number of different forms. The more common schemes usually involve addressing envelopes from one's home. A Philadelphia con man was indicted on charges on mail fraud for operating such a swindle.[51] He took his victims for more than $60,000. In another similar work-at-home swindle, consumers were solicited to invest in a work-at-home-type track tape cartridge operation.[52] Kits were sold to them for $4000 each. They were told that the promoters would repurchase their completed tapes. Some of the victims never received the kits, while others were unable to find buyers for the finished product. The promoters did not repurchase them as promised.

Franchise and pyramid schemes are very similar to the business operation frauds.[53] Franchise frauds usually involve misrepresentations regarding the earnings and business viability of franchises. These schemes have increased steadily with the rise of the franchise industry. Investors are assured of discounts for supplies and are promised training and advertising. Often these promises are simply not kept. Franchises may be sold in various areas of our economy. Interestingly, a firm with a dubious reputation recently advertised the sale of franchises in the idea-promotion field for sums ranging from $20,000 to $50,000.[54]

One of the better known pyramid schemes involved a Florida promoter and his Dare To Be Great Company. The firm and its officers were charged by the federal government with mail fraud and conspiracy for attempting to defraud thousands of consumers out of their money. The promoters had induced investors to purchase multilevel distributorships for the sale of cosmetics and self-improvement courses, with promises of possible earnings in the area of $50,000 to $200,000 a year. The victims paid fees for the distributorships.[55] A similar scheme involved a Connecticut firm that charged investors more than $20,000 each.[56]

In a pyramid swindle, the investor is promised large profits for an initial, small investment of money and labor. He is given the right to sell a product, usually manufactured by the promoters, within a designated geographic area. His profits usually come not from selling the product, but rather from selling low-level distributorships to other investors. Cosmetics, clothes, burglar alarms, books, and even correspondence courses have been marketed in pyramid schemes. Unfortunately, the investor eventually loses his investment as the pool of potential investors dries up. These swindles can usually be identified by promises of large profits and by franchises in poorly defined geographic areas. In addition, most advertise that the investor needs no experience. In most cases, the investor expects to make his profit not from selling the product but from selling parts of his franchise to other investors.[57]

Merchandising frauds are also a serious consumer problem. They account for millions of dollars lost annually by the public. These swindles take on various forms, such as false and misleading mail order solicitations.[58] These may claim that quality goods are available for a short period of time at a discount price, when in fact the promoters have no intention of supplying the quality products, but rather inferior ones. At times, the promoters may just take the money and run, returning nothing at all. Contest frauds are also part of this swindle, and consumers are usually invited to partake in this contest at no charge. In return for a chance to win a prize, they are asked to try out a product or service. Usually, the winners have been preselected and the contest is a sham.

Several years ago, a New York firm became the subject of a national investigation.[59] The firm researched old bank records for unclaimed accounts; once these were located, the firm would contact, by mail, individuals who had the same surname as that of the deceased owner of the account. Those contacted were informed that they could be the legal heirs of these accounts, and that for a small advance fee, the firm would supply the individual with a report on the account. The firm, however, failed to disclose that the likelihood of recovery was virtually nonexistent, and that the same letter may have also been sent to other individuals. In another case, the president of a firm was indicted for allegedly defrauding investors of more than $1 million.[60] The firm falsely represented to these investors that it had signed contracts to feed several million school children, and that it had developed a freezer-oven that would revolutionize the food industry.

Advanced-fee swindles are not new. They can be traced to the eighteenth century. However, they began to increase dramatically in size and quantity after the Korean war. They are particularly prevalent in times of economic recession.[61] The objective of the scheme is to obtain fees in advance for products or services that the con men have no intention of providing, or that they provide in limited quantity. Advertisements may be placed in large newspapers, indicating that the firm has millions of dollars readily available for loans to businessmen and others in need of financing. In return, the firm may request, through its agents, 10 percent of the intended loan as an advance fee. To reassure the borrower that the firm is financially sound and that the operation is indeed legitimate, the agents may supply him with false financial statements. The applicant may also be told that before the loan can be made, his business must first be surveyed by an agent of the firm—for a fee, of course. To further placate the nervous borrower, the promoters may place his advance fee in an escrow account. The account can later be raped through various elaborate schemes. Consumers and other borrowers have been taken for millions of dollars by such schemes.

Consumer frauds are numerous, and increasing annually. The new technology and the changing economic environment (such as the energy crisis) give rise to newer and more elaborate swindles that victimize the consuming public out of billions of dollars each year. The preceding are only a minute, though admittedly important, facet of consumer fraud. Warranty frauds are also widespread, as are repair frauds, measurement frauds, commercial-credit frauds, and chain-referral swindles. The problem is expanding rapidly, the result in large part of the failure of law enforcement to respond effectively to the challenge of consumer frauds. In addition, most legal action takes the form of civil suits, with the results usually being injunctions or small fines, or both. The great majority of these actions culminate in consent decrees—without the defendant admitting to any wrongdoing. Generally, it must be said that this area of fraud is made possible not only by the naiveté of the consuming public, but also by the failure of prosecutors, judges, and legislators to act decisively.[62]

Notes

1. "Minneapolis County Attorney and Minnesota Attorney General File Joint Consumer Lawsuit," *National District Attorneys Association Economic Crime Digest* (November-December 1975):13.

2. Ibid., p. 19.

3. "President of Truck Driving School Convicted in Philadelphia," *National District Attorneys Association Economic Crime Digest* (August-October 1975):170.

4. Chamber of Commerce of the United States, *White Collar Crime* (Washington, D.C.: Chamber of Commerce of the United States, 1974), p. 6.

5. Gerald F. Seib, "Dallas Ordinance Against Fraud in Car Repairs Helps Consumers Recover Nearly $3,000 a Month," *Wall Street Journal*, September 13, 1977, p. 46.

6. Chamber of Commerce of the United States, *White Collar Crime*, p. 26.

7. *Shea* v. *United States*, 251 F.440 (1918).

8. 18 U.S.C., secs. 1341, 1342.

9. 18 U.S.C., sec. 1343.

10. *Sellinger* v. *Freeway Mobile Home Sales*, 521 P.2d 1119 (1974).

11. *Rice* v. *Snarlin*, 266 N.E.2d 183 (1970).

12. *Scott* v. *Western International Surplus Sales, Inc.*, 517 P.2d 661 (1974).

13. Economic Crime Project of the National District Attorneys Association, *Fighting the $40 Billion Rip-Off* (Chicago, Ill.: National District Attorneys Association, 1976), p. 6.

14. "Home Improvements," *National District Attorneys Association Economic Crime Digest* (March-April-May 1975):20.

15. "Home Improvement," *National District Attorneys Association Economic Crime Digest* (May-June-July 1974):175.

16. *United States* v. *Caine*, 441 F.2d 454 (1971).

17. "Energy Crisis Frauds," *National District Attorneys Association Economic Crime Digest* (December 1974):337, 338.

18. Public Citizens Staff Report, *White Collar Crime* (Washington, D.C.: Congress Watch, 1974), pp. 170, 171.

19. "Merchandising Frauds," *National District Attorneys Association Economic Crime Digest* (May-June-July 1974):170.

20. Ibid., pp. 170, 171.

21. "New San Francisco Fraud Unit Sues National Housing Rental Agency," *National District Attorneys Association Economic Crime Digest* (March-April 1976):104.

22. "Health Spa Trade Rules Proposed by FTC," *National District Attorneys Association Economic Crime Digest* (August-October 1975):149, 150.

23. N.Y. Gen. Bus. Law, sec. 350(a).

24. New York Penal Law, sec. 190.20.

25. Calif. Bus. & Prof. Code, sec. 17500; and N.Y. Gen. Bus. Law, sec. 349(g).

26. 15 U.S.C., secs. 52(a), 52(b).

27. *Federal Trade Commission* v. *Colgate-Palmolive Company*, 380 U.S. 374 (1965).

28. Practising Law Institute, *Consumer Credit 1975* (New York: Practising Law Institute, 1975), p. 19.

29. *People ex. rel.* v. *Gym of America, Inc.*, 493 P.2d 660 (1972).

30. "Land Sales," *National District Attorneys Association Economic Crime Digest* (May-June-July 1974):172, 173.

31. "Floridians Bilked of $350 Million," *National District Attorneys Association Economic Crime Digest* (March-April-May 1975):24, 25.

32. "AMREP, Inc., Indicted in New York," *National District Attorneys Association Economic Crime Digest* (August-October 1975):153.

33. Calif. Bus. & Prof. Code, sec. 11010.

34. 15 U.S.C., sec. 1701.

35. *Village Development* v. *Filice*, 526 P.2d 83 (1974).

36. Ibid., p. 83.

37. "Charity Frauds," *National District Attorneys Association Economic Crime Digest* (May-June-July 1974):182.

38. "The Busy Banker of Sark Turns to Consulting On Swindles," *National District Attorneys Association Economic Crime Digest* (August-October 1975):146.

39. *Koolish* v. *United States*, 340 F.2d 513 (1965).

40. "Baltimore and Professional Fundraisers," *National District Attorneys Association Economic Crime Digest* (June-July 1975):79, 80.

41. *State by Head* v. *Aamco Auto Transmission, Inc.*, 199 N.W.2d 444 (1972).

42. "Mileage Rollbacks," *National District Attorneys Association Economic Crime Digest* (October-November 1974):282.

43. "Employment/Vanity Business," *National District Attorneys Association Economic Crime Digest* (May-June-July 1974):168.

44. "Vocational Schools," *National District Attorneys Association Economic Crime Digest* (August-September 1974):222, 223.

45. *Adams* v. *United States*, 347 F.2d 665 (1965).

46. "FTC Issues Orders Against Psychic Surgery Tours," *National District Attorneys Association Economic Crime Digest* (August-October 1975):151.

47. *Kugler* v. *Haitian Tours, Inc.*, 293 A.2d 706 (1967).

48. "Idea Promotions," *National District Attorneys Association Economic Crime Digest* (August-September 1974):217.

49. "Idea Promotions," *National District Attorneys Association Economic Crime Digest* (May-June-July 1974):163-165.

50. Chamber of Commerce of the United States, *White Collar Crime*, p. 27.

51. "Idea Promotions," *National District Attorneys Association Economic Crime Digest* (August-September 1974):221.

52. Ibid.

53. *Crooks* v. *United States*, 179 F.2d 304 (1950); *Irwin* v. *United States*, 338 F.2d 770 (1964).

54. "Idea Promotion," *National District Attorneys Association Economic Crime Digest* (August-September 1974):218.

55. Note, "Pyramid Schemes: Dare-to-be-Regulated," *Geo. L.J.* 61 (1973):1257.

56. "Use of Probability and Statistics in Prosecuting Pyramid Fraud Cases," *National District Attorneys Association Economic Crime Digest* (March-April 1976):119, 120.

57. See *Gallion* v. *Alabama Market Centers, Inc.*, 213 So.2d 841 (1968); and *Florida Discount Centers, Inc.,* v. *Antinori*, 226 So.2d 693 (1970).

58. See *United States* v. *Press*, 336 F.2d 1003 (1964); and *United States* v. *Bloom*, 237 F.2d 158 (1956).

59. "Advance Fee," *National District Attorneys Association Economic Crime Digest* (March-April-May 1975):34-36.

60. "Advance-Fee Scheme Indicted in D.C.," *National District Attorneys Association Economic Crime Digest* (August-October 1975):154.

61. See *United States* v. *Dorfman*, 335 F.Supp. 675 (1971).

62. For a review of attempts to remedy the present federal regulatory system, see John A. Jenkins, "Buddy Can You Spare a Nickel?" *Student Lawyer* (October 1977):23.

8

Frauds in Government Contracts and Programs

A recent Congressional investigation has disclosed that certain physicians performed twice as many operations on individuals receiving Medicaid benefits as they did on non-Medicaid patients.[1] The cost of Medicaid surgery is presently put at $7 billion a year. In a major Eastern city, prosecutors were investigating allegations that a welfare family, which had received more than $200,000 in assistance payments, may have defrauded the program out of more than $40,000.[2] The investigators were looking into a series of fires that may have been set by the family, as well as loss and relocation claims filed by them with the city welfare department.

In Washington, D.C., federal investigators were acting on charges that a $3 million a year contract for computer services given to a private firm may have been the result of gratuities provided to federal employees by that firm.[3] At least one federal employee may have received gifts and free entertainment from the firm. In another part of the country, the developer of a $50 million office and apartment complex, as well as the mayor of the city, were indicted by a federal grand jury.[4] The indictment accused the developer of paying more than $400,000 in bribes to local politicians.

In 1950 the cost of social services, for both the federal and local government, was approximately $23 billion annually; defense-related spendings for that same year were about $12 billion.[5] Presently, those same costs are in the area of $375 billion and $100 billion, respectively.[6] It is estimated that by 1980, those costs will increase to $550 billion and $130 billion each.[7] The cost of government medical and social programs alone has increased more than 100 percent in the last several years. In addition, 178 federal agencies have paid over $900 million, in one year alone, in fees to outside consultants involved in the numerous federal programs and contracts presently in force.[8]

The cost of government contracts and programs, both at the federal and state level, is on the increase. At present, the government is the largest consumer in this country. Like any member of the consuming public, it is open to fraud. Government contracts and programs have become the targets of criminal activity, ranging from the individual criminal to some of this nation's largest businesses, to members of organized crime itself. Frauds in government contracts and programs may well jeopardize many of our important social and economic institutions. The recent increase in such frauds is cause for alarm.

Defining the Contractual Relationship

Under Article I, Section 9, of the U.S. Constitution, only Congress has the power to appropriate funds from the Treasury; only Congress can legislate as to how the Executive Branch of government must employ those funds. Congress also establishes rules and regulations concerning government contracts and programs. The United States government, under the law, can contract for services and materials like any private citizen; it can also be sued and held liable under the law like any private citizen.[9] However, no government contract can exceed expenditures allocated for that purpose. Unlike the private individual, the federal government contracts as an agent on behalf of the national interest. The funds it allocates for various services and needs must not exceed appropriations set for those specific objectives. If the funds are excessive, the government then violates those rules which were established to guide its contracting needs.

The government, like any private corporation, contracts through its agents; these, in turn, must act within the scope of their authorization. If they exceed that scope, then the government can challenge contracts signed by them on its behalf. The contract itself differs little, save for clauses and provisions characteristic of the specific needs of government, from an agreement between private parties. It has, as do private contracts, two key provisions: (1) there must be an offer for a service or goods, and (2) an acceptance by a second party to perform and provide those services or goods. Once an offer is accepted, the agreement is binding and the contract is enforceable in a court of law.

Government offers to contract are made in one of two ways: (1) by advertisement or (2) by negotiations. When the former procedure is employed, the government issues an invitation for bids to the private sector; the invitation also describes the minimum needs of the government. Qualified bidders then submit sealed bids; all bids must be in by a specified time, and they are opened on a designated date. The lowest bidder whose bid conforms to the needs of the government will then be given the contract. The clear purpose of this route is to open the process to the competitive market and thus secure the services or goods at the lowest possible cost. The process also has as its objective the safeguarding of government contracts from favoritism, collusion, graft, and other fraudulent practices.

When the head of an agency determines that advertising is not the best route, the government will then negotiate with one or more parties for its needs. This process also seeks to address itself to the problems connected with graft and favoritism, and the bidder is asked to submit one or more proposals. However, this route tends to be less formal, and procedures are less well defined. Heads of agencies are allowed a greater degree of flexibility than they enjoy in the advertising route.

To insulate the bidding process from fraud, numerous statutes, rules, and regulations have been passed. For example, members of Congress are prohibited from benefiting from government contracts; criminal penalties are provided for those found guilty of violating this statute.[10] Payoffs and kickbacks to government employees, whether by the bidding party or by an agent of his, for award of a government contract are illegal and can be prosecuted criminally.[11] The government can also bring civil suit to recover damages. National defense contracts provide for the termination of the contractor's right to proceed if it is found that the latter offered any gratuities to government officials with the objective of securing the contract.[12] In cases where there is collusion in the bidding process, the government agency is directed to refer the matter to the Justice Department for prosecution.[13] In cases involving a conflict of interest, such as where the government agent has a financial interest in the outcome of the bidding process, this matter should be brought to the attention of the head of the agency; further, the party who has the conflict should exclude himself from the contracting process. Criminal and civil sanctions are available when this is not done.[14]

Although statutes have been enacted to insulate the contracting process from fraud, and although rules have been established to open the process to all qualified members of the public, actual practice is to the contrary. Frauds have been on the increase; billions of dollars have been paid annually for shoddy work, nonexistent services, and "ghost" consultants. In large part, this has been a product of lax enforcement of present rules and regulations, a lack of built-in safeguards in many government programs, and a lack of fervor on the part of prosecutors to bring to court politically and economically powerful groups.

Frauds in Government Contracts

Abuses in this area are common, and take on various forms. They may involve collusion in bidding, kickbacks and payoffs to government officials, campaign contributions to political figures, delivery of shoddy work, cost overruns, filing of false claims for nonexistent services, padding the cost of material, hiring of friends and associates who formerly worked in government, offering inducements to government officials, and many others. Human ingenuity has proven its ability, when combined with a receptive environment, to easily circumvent the rules and regulations designed to prevent this very form of behavior.

Kickbacks and payoffs are so common that in one city alone they amount to $75 million annually.[15] In another city, the mayor and his associates took in more than $1 million in kickbacks from the local construction industry doing business with the city.[16] The rigging of bids is so prevalent that it affects the entire spectrum of the government-contract arena. Investigators, for example, have looked into the rigging of bids in the U.S. Food and Peace Program by several grain companies.[17] Cost overruns in national defense contracts have been so common that a high naval officer has charged that contractors are intentionally "inflating" claims in the millions of dollars.[18] In a somewhat related case, a federal grand jury has indicted a large defense contractor on charges that it fraudulently overcharged the government by more than $30 million.[19]

In 1953 Congress passed the Small Business Act;[20] the act established the Small Business Administration (SBA). The objective of the act was to ensure that small firms would also be allocated a fair proportion of government contracts; the SBA was to assist them in so doing. The act empowered the SBA to enter into contracts with government agencies and then arrange for small businesses (subcontractors) to perform these services. To qualify under this program, a small firm must be first certified by the SBA. There are two ways in which a small firm can apply for qualification. First, it must certify in its offer (to act as subcontractor) that it does qualify as a small firm; and unless a competitor challenges that certification within five days of the opening of the bid, the SBA will so qualify it. Or second, it can apply to an SBA regional office for a small business certificate. In large part, the SBA will take the applicant at his word; no background investigations are conducted to determine the veracity of the applicant's statements. These lax measures undoubtedly encourage frauds.

The act has also been used in the last several years to assist minority businesses; these are known as Section 8(a) program participants.[21] There are presently more than 500 small firms employed in over 1000 Section 8(a) programs around the country. These programs, valued at more than $300 million, have been riddled with fraud. Large corporate contractors have set up shell firms, which they totally control, to qualify as subcontractors for government contracts under the Small Business Act. Programs established to assist small minority-owned businesses have become their targets. White-controlled firms (also called "fronts") have siphoned off millions of dollars in SBA contracts by simply hiring blacks as executive officers.[22] For example, an elderly black farm laborer was a director (front) for three small firms and secretary-treasurer for a fourth firm; these firms had been granted millions of dollars in government contracts by the SBA.[23] When questioned by federal investigators, the elderly laborer said he did not know what these firms did. In another case, another black man was made president and chairman of the board of another small business; as a result, the firm qualified under the Section 8(a) program (minorities) and was given a $1 million government contract. When questioned by government investigators, he told them that he only signed the firm's blank checks and did not really know what the company did.

Payoffs many times take the form of political contributions. For example, in a recent trial, a former corporate officer testified that his employer had made a $205,000 cash payment to a former U.S. President, a $100,000 payment to the former chairman of one of our national political parties, and an average of $400,000 in annual payments to various political figures.[24] His employer was a large defense contractor.

Frauds in Government Programs

Abuses in this area usually involve the numerous social service programs such as welfare, food stamps, social security, Medicare and Medicaid, nursing homes, and the many new and growing areas of government involvement in social and economic assistance to the needy, elderly, and young. Many of these frauds are characterized by false claims, ghost payrolls, nepotism, collusion, and other abuses. The cost to the public in terms of funds siphoned off by these operators runs into the billions of dollars annually.

The annual cost of welfare programs for one large city alone approaches $4 billion, with a bureaucracy of more than 20,000 employees to administer it and more than 10 percent of that city's residents being its recipients.[25] The number of unqualified individuals who take advantage of these welfare programs is estimated to be in the tens of thousands. In the Washington, D.C. area alone, over 1000 federal employees have been identified by government computers as receiving welfare payments; more than one third of these were earning over $10,000 annually in salaries.[26] One recent Congressional inquiry found that as many as 19 percent of all recipients of the Aid to Families with Dependent Children (welfare) Program may have been ineligible; more than $500 million annually was being misspent in this program as a result.[27]

The federal government has allocated more than $4 billion to food stamps, which are exchanged as currency in more than 200,000 retail establishments in return for food purchases.[28] Investigators, however, have uncovered numerous frauds that run into the millions of dollars annually. For example, two clerics recently admitted in federal court that they had swindled the program out of more than $200,000.[29] With these funds they bought private homes, an ice cream parlor, and took several vacation trips. This, however, is only the tip of the iceberg. Food stamps are presently being employed to purchase narcotics, they are being counterfeited, and a large black market has evolved around them that runs into the millions of dollars.

Assistance programs have also proven lucrative targets for white-collar felons. For example, the federal government, through its Bureau of Indian Affairs (BIA) and other channels, funnels more than $100 million annually to the 480 Indian tribes in this country. In one case, four members of an Oklahoma tribe bilked the tribe out of more than $500,000 in federal funds.[30] Not to be outdone, a group of felons swindled an Arizona tribe out of more than $13 million.[31] Investigators have found that some of these funds have also been used to pay personal bills and even bankroll gambling junkets.

In one New York case, a state senator and four other individuals were indicted by a federal grand jury on charges of conspiring to defraud the federal government.[32] The defendants had set up a shell corporation. Through it, they purchased some real estate for $75,000, which was then resold to one of the antipoverty agencies in the South Bronx for $350,000; they realized a quick profit of $275,000. In addition, these defendants were also charged with having misappropriated antipoverty funds. One defendant was also charged with having lied to a federal grand jury.

A Congressional subcommittee found that the antipoverty programs were being run incompetently, and that these programs were also marred by numerous abuses and nepotism.[33] The Community Services Administration, with an annual budget of several hundred million dollars, came under serious attack. The agency was established in 1974 to take over the antipoverty programs from the Office of Economic Opportunity. The Congressional investigators found that the new agency had spent more than $20 million in questionable ways; in at least one case, salaries were paid to employees who provided no services to the agency.

The federal health care program, with a $15 billion annual budget, is also riddled with fraud; as much as $1 billion annually may be involved in questionable expenditures.[34] More than 40,000 doctors and pharmacists may have been engaged in improper practices, with more than $200 million in Medicaid claims improperly paid to doctors. Investigators have found, for example, that one physician billed Medicaid for 43 comprehensive examinations involving only one patient.[35] Another physician billed Medicaid for 42 lab tests for each of his 225 patients in an 11-month period.[36] Investigators have also found that physicians overcharge the Medicare and Medicaid programs by as much as 400 percent.[37] One Texas physician was found to have submitted more than 60 false claims; a Missouri dentist submitted a claim for a prostate ailment; and one New Jersey physician billed the Medicare program more than $10,000 for removing "malignant tumors" that were really harmless warts.[38]

Although investigators continue to unravel sophisticated frauds in government programs, prosecutions are lax and punishment meted out against the guilty is usually no more than a "slap on the wrist." Investigators have uncovered more than 40,000 allegations of fraud and abuse in the Medicare program alone in the last several years. Of these, only 220 resulted in successful prosecution, with only 37 offenders going to prison.[39]

For example, two physicians found guilty of filing false Medicaid claims were given suspended sentences; they could have received sentences of up to 205 years for the offenses involved.[40] In another case, a group of convicted felons who defrauded a large city of more than $500,000 in antipoverty funds were described as "nice guys." In contrast, a defendant convicted of attempted robbery in Washington, D.C. was recently given an 18-year prison sentence.[41]

Although investigators continue to unravel complex frauds in both the government contracts and programs areas, prosecutors continue to lag in prosecution. Many cases that are referred to the Justice Department for criminal action never surface again; few ever reach the courtroom. Further, with those which do finally reach this stage and result in a conviction, the usual disposition is probation or a suspended sentence. For example, from a group of 82 individuals convicted of a white-collar offense in the District of Columbia, more than half received probation or a suspended sentence.[42]

If the growing problem of fraud in government contracts and programs is to be curtailed, meaningful enforcement measures and built-in safeguards must be devised and implemented. At present, both are sadly lacking. As a result, the American taxpayer continues to pay billions of dollars annually to swindlers.

Notes

1. Richard D. Lyons, "Medicaid Patients Undergo Surgery Twice as Often," *Washington Star*, September 1, 1977, p. A-2.

2. "Arson Suspects Got Fire Aid," *Washington Post*, July 26, 1977, p. A-7.

3. "U.S. Expands Inquiry of On-Line Systems' Government Contracts," *Wall Street Journal*, August 15, 1977, p. 10.

4. "Hawaii Prosecutor Doubts Indictments of a Witness Will Delay Mayor's Trial," *New York Times*, September 1, 1977, p. 34.

5. "Social Welfare Spending—Can Anyone Bring It Under Control," *U.S. News & World Report*, March 14, 1977, pp. 40-42.

6. Ibid., p. 41.

7. Ibid.

8. Bill Peterson, "Outsiders a Big Part of U.S. Payroll," *Washington Post*, August 7, 1977, p. A-3; see also, John D. Hanrahau, *Government For Sale* (Washington, D.C.: American Federation of State, County and Municipal Employees, 1977), pp. 1-11.

9. *United States* v. *Allegheny County*, 322 U.S. 174 (1942).

10. 18 U.S.C., 431.

11. 41 U.S.C., 51.

12. 10 U.S.C., 2207.

13. 10 U.S.C., 2305; and 41 U.S.C., 252.

14. Ibid.; and also 10 U.S.C., 2306; and 41 U.S.C., 254.

15. Standards and Goals Commission, "Integrity in Government," in *Theft of the City*, John A. Gardiner and David J. Olson, eds. (Bloomington, Indiana: Indiana Univ. Press, 1974), pp. 238-239.

16. Fred J. Cook, "Who Rules New Jersey?" in *Theft of a City*, p. 73.

17. "Grand Jury Studies Possible Rigging of Grain Firm Bids," *Wall Street Journal*, January 28, 1977, p. 26.

18. "Rickover Asks Hill Help on Shipbuilders Claims," *Washington Post*, March 25, 1977, p. A-9.

19. Jane Seaberry, "Litton Is Indicted in $37 Million Overcharge Case," *Washington Post*, April 7, 1977, p. A-1.

20. 15 U.S.C., 631.

21. Section 8(a) programs have been employed to allocate subcontracts to minority-owned firms.

22. John M. Gosko, "Whites Reap SBA Aid to Minorities," *Washington Post*, July 4, 1977, p. A-1.

23. John M. Gosko, "Abuses Found in Minority Business Aid," *Washington Post*, May 30, 1977, pp. A-1, A-15.

24. "Hughes Tied to Politics," *Washington Post*, December 4, 1977, p. A-18.

25. William Claborne, "For Mayor Welfare Help Isn't Coming Soon," *Washington Post*, August 7, 1977, p. A-14.

26. Milton Coleman, "Federal Workers on D.C. Welfare, Califano Says," *Washington Post*, September 20, 1977, p. A-1.

27. "AFDC Audit Shows $550 Million Misspent," *Washington Post*, August 5, 1977, p. A-12.

28. John V. Graziano, "Department of Agriculture: The Third Largest Criminal Investigative Force in the Federal Government," *Police Chief* (July 1975):54-55.

29. Timothy S. Robinson and Alice Bonner, "Two Clerics Admit Swindling $250,000 from Food Stamps," *Washington Post*, August 7, 1976, pp. A-1, A-6.

30. Robert L. Sunison, "White Collar Crime Rises on the Reservations as More U.S. Money Is Channeled to the Tribes," *Wall Street Journal*, September 9, 1977, p. 30.

31. Ibid.

32. Howard Blum, "U.S. Jury Indicts Galiber and Four on Fraud Charges," *New York Times*, pp. 1, 49.

33. Warren Brown, "Antipoverty Agency Reported Riddled with Waste and Fraud," *Washington Post*, August 12, 1977, p. A-14.

34. Helen Dewar, "Medicaid Throwaway: $1 Billion a Year," *Washington Post*, October 17, 1977, p. A-1.

35. Richard L. Lyons, "Two House Subcommittees Seek Health Fraud Curb," *Washington Post*, March 4, 1977, p. A-3.

36. Ibid.

37. Victor Coln, "Lab Testing Charges Inflated, GAO Claims," *Burlington Free Press*, July 28, 1977, p. 8.

38. Nancy Hicks, "Total of Medicare Fraud Put at $300 Million a Year," *New York Times*, July 29, 1977, p. 15.

39. Based on my interviews with government investigators and prosecutors.

40. Nancy Hicks, "Total of Medicare Fraud Put at $300 Million a Year," p. 15.

41. Based on interviews with Mr. Waverly A. Yates, Executive Director, Bonabond, Inc., Washington, D.C., during September 1977.

42. Robert W. Ogren, "The Ineffectiveness of the Criminal Sanction in Fraud and Corruption Cases: Losing the Battle Against White Collar Crime," *The American Criminal Law Review* XI (1973):962.

Insurance Frauds

A ring of more than 100 individuals, many of them students from several Middle Eastern nations, is said to have filed more than $1 million in false insurance claims against a number of American insurance firms.[1] In one state alone, insurance companies may have paid the ring more than $250,000 in claims. The group is well organized and operates nationally. Its members are trained in techniques of staging phony accidents and fake injuries. Arson claims alone have run into the millions of dollars. Investigators fear that some of this money may have been used to finance guerilla operations in the Middle East.[2]

In another case, two officers of a large Chicago-based firm pleaded guilty to charges of mail fraud involving an arson scheme.[3] The defendants were charged with having falsified their insurance claims. Investigators found that the defendants had inflated the value of the plant's machinery, as well as the firm's sales figures. The sentencing judge, however, placed both individuals on probation.

Insurance fraud runs into several million dollars annually; one source places the figure at over $2 billion per year. Unfortunately, insurance companies are not the only losers. Policyholders can also be the targets of these frauds. One such case concerned more than a dozen union trust funds.[4] The scheme involved a group of insurance firms that took in more than $30 million in insurance premiums from these unions. Investigators note that at least $10 million of these premiums was misused, with little chance of recovery by the insured.

Understanding the World of Insurance

The modern insurance industry is an outgrowth of the needs of mercantile Europe. It became customary in seventeenth century England for those who were interested in insuring their vessels and goods to meet at Lloyd's Coffee House in London.[5] Here both insured and insurer met. The latter usually consisted of a syndicate of several individuals, each sharing part of the profits along with the possibility of loss. In the eighteenth century, these underwriters formalized their association and adopted what has come to be known as the Lloyd policy. In the latter part of the nineteenth century, the underwriters formed the Lloyd's Corporation. The organization does not actually sell insurance, but rather sets policy and enacts rules by which its members abide. Similar in some respects to our stock exchanges, it affords both the insurer and insured a meeting place and provides for rules to govern the relationship.[6]

By the twentieth century, the insurance industry had grown in complexity and sophistication, and insurers themselves began to take various forms. However, associations similar to that of Lloyd's of London are few in the United States. Local legislation has limited their growth. Nevertheless, both stock companies and fraternal associations have played a role in the insurance industry. Stock companies are owned by stockholders, but they are not liable for the company's losses beyond their own investments. Fraternal associations have also made their way into the insurance world. But unlike the Lloyd groups and the stock companies, the fraternal groups are non-profit and are organized for the benefit of the members. These associations provide insurance at a discount to their members. Many of these groups, however, have failed financially—due, in part, to bad business judgment and fraud.

One of the more common forms of insuring entities is the mutual company.[7] These companies began to play an important role at the turn of the century, and many are now incorporated, as is the case with stock companies. Unlike the latter, however, mutual insurers both insure and pass the burden of insurance to the insured. They dominate the life insurance business. In theory, at least, they operate for the benefit of their policyholders. Many of these companies are usually controlled and dominated by management and have been victimized through fraud schemes.

The insurance industry has expanded rapidly in the last century. The earlier forms of insurance usually involved fire, marine, casualty, and life. The early statutes usually restricted an insurer to one of these areas. Although some jurisdictions allowed insurers to engage in multi-insurance sales, many firms continue to specialize in one or more of these areas. Fire insurance has expanded to cover damage from civil disturbance, explosions, and earthquakes. Marine insurance has expanded to include inland shipping. Casualty insurance has expanded to include workmen's compensation, accident, and health, as well as credit insurance.

Life insurance continues to dominate the field and now includes various personal, accident, and health policies, as well as an array of life insurance trusts. Our modern industrial society has also given rise to numerous industry-related insurance policies. The insurance industry, at present, is a powerful force in our economy.[8] It is an industry fraught with the potential for vast frauds, and one that for many years has escaped the close scrutiny of national watchdogs. Insurance fraud is on the increase. All facets of the industry are presently under attack. The criminal may take the guise of an insured or insurer, preying on the public at large or on the stockholders of the firm. The insurance industry is an extremely vulnerable structure and invites criminal attack at every level.

Insurance Law

An insurance agreement may be defined as a contract between the insurer and insured, whereby the former agrees to assume the latter's risk of loss in consideration for the payment of a premium.[9] There are four key elements to every insurance contract; and without any one of these, the contract is void: (1) there must be an offer and an acceptance; (2) there must be consideration; (3) the parties to the contract must have the capacity to enter into such an agreement; and (4) the subject matter insured must be legal. An absence of any of these four elements may lead to civil litigation but does not give rise to criminal prosecution.

An insurance contract need not be in writing to be enforceable. It can be oral, provided that it is made by a party with authority to enter into such an agreement. In addition to the insured and the insurer, every contract has a third party, the beneficiary. The latter is the individual for whose benefit the risk has been assumed. The insured risk, however, must not occur as a result of the intentional act of the insured. If it does, as where the insured plans an arson fraud, the insurer need not pay and the insured can be liable in both civil and criminal law. The exception is where the insured commits the intentional act while not in control of his senses, as, for example, when he is intoxicated or insane.

The insured, in the absence of fraud, is said to accept his insurance policy regardless of whether he has read it or not. However, where the insurance contract is not clearly expressed, it is construed according to the intent of the individuals involved and usually in favor of the insured. Often the insured will complain that he has been defrauded by the insurer, but there are situations under which the latter need not live up to the insurance contract. For example, when the insured fails to pay his premiums, the insurer is excused from payment under the contract. A state of war may also excuse the insurer from honoring its obligations. If the insurer is insolvent (provided the result is not a product of fraud), it will serve to excuse the insurer. A waiver of the premium by the insurer because of the incapacity of the insured or a waiver of prompt payment by the insured will also serve to excuse the insurer. The insured may find civil remedies in some of these cases, but prosecutors will decline criminal prosecution of the insurer.

An insurance contract may be cancelled either by agreement or by an act of the parties. The parties may jointly agree to terminate a contract, or in some instances, the insurance contracts may provide for termination by one of the parties. However, the cancelling party must first give notice of cancellation to the other party for the cancellation to be effective. If either the insured or the insurer discovers that it was coerced into entering the contract by fraudulent representations, then it may be allowed to rescind the agreement. If a third party has an interest in the agreement, it must consent to the cancellation of the contract; otherwise, the agreement will remain unaffected.

Misrepresentations in the making of an insurance contract can void that contract and, when made intentionally, can result in criminal prosecution. However, the misrepresentation must have induced either of the parties to enter the contract. Further, it must be material in nature. If intentional, it can involve a criminal violation of law. It must be a misstatement of either past or present facts, upon which the insurance contract is based. For example, a ring of eight individuals was uncovered in Los Angeles and prosecuted for filing false claims with insurance firms in that area.[10] The ring staged more than 60 accidents, claiming damages and injuries. The defendants had also created a phony company to bolster their false claims. Nevertheless, the fraud must be material to the risk that is insured.

Concealment of material facts may also result in fraud. However, two elements must exist: (1) the party must conceal a material fact; and (2) it must do so with the intent to defraud the other party to the contract. The test of materiality is: Would the fact, if known to the other party, lead the latter to reject the contract? For example, if the insured disclosed to the insurer his scheme and the insurer is foolish enough to go ahead and enter the contract, it cannot be said that the insured has defrauded it by filing false claims. By the same token, if the insurer discloses its scheme to the insured and the latter suffers losses, it cannot be said that it was defrauded. It voluntarily entered the agreement, fully aware of all material facts. However, the majority of cases that involve either concealment or misrepresentation usually involve policyholders; they culminate in civil remedies rather than criminal action. For example, a policyholder who conceals his ill health from the insurer will not be prosecuted. The insurer will simply refuse to honor the policy. It is difficult to prove the actual intent of the policyholder in this case. Further, the practice is so common that criminal prosecution would only serve to inundate the courts with unimportant cases. However, when an insurer conceals or misstates its financial situation, many policyholders may lose large sums of their investment, and the fraud may culminate in criminal prosecution.

An insurer can be held liable for the acts of its agent, provided the latter acted under instructions from the former. There are three categories of agents in the insurance industry. The *general agent* is the first category; he represents the insurer and is usually delegated broad powers. He can execute contracts on behalf of the insurer, and the insurer can be held civilly liable for his actions (provided he acts within the scope of his duties).

A second category is the *special agent*. He may solicit contracts on behalf of the insurer, but his authority is limited and dependent on the final approval of the insurer. In a criminal case, the actions of a special agent will not necessarily result in criminal prosecution of the insurer unless the latter condoned and conspired with the former.

A third category is the *broker*. He usually acts as the agent of the insured, but brokers have been known to scheme with policyholders in frauds against the insurer. However, when the broker delivers the contract to the insured or the first payment to the insurer, he may be acting as an agent of the latter. Brokers can thus be involved in frauds perpetrated by either the insured or the insurer.

The major thrust of insurance law is in the civil arena. There is little concern with criminal behavior. Even misrepresentations and acts of concealment are handled more in terms of their impact on the insurance agreement rather than with regard to possible criminal violations. Insurance law shows little concern for the frauds that have permeated the industry. In addition to the insurer, insured, and beneficiary, the public also has a stake in the outcome of these agreements. It bears the cost of fraud in terms of higher premiums. In instances of blatant fraud, both civil and criminal sanctions should be employed. Insurance frauds are usually the acts of sophisticated felons, and a new approach is needed to deal with them.

Categories of Frauds

Insurance swindles can take any one of the following three forms: (1) frauds by policyholders against the insurer, (2) frauds by the insurer against the public, and (3) frauds by management against the public. The first category usually involves false claims against the insurer and may encompass life, marine, fire, and casualty insurance. The policyholder may be an individual or another corporation; an insider may also be involved, who assists and arranges to have the false claims honored. The fraud could involve a well-organized national gang, which stages phony accidents and injuries and then files false claims with the unsuspecting insurer.

Frauds against insurance companies account for over $1 billion annually.[11] They range from false death claims[12] to such complicated schemes as the osteopath who purchased insurance from more than 30 firms and filed false claims with each.[13] In one major urban center, more than 70 individuals were involved in an ambulance-chasing scheme.[14] The group included doctors, lawyers, private investigators, and even policemen who acted as runners. The latter directed the victims to these lawyers and doctors in return for kickbacks. Another ring, operating out of a New England urban center, defrauded insurers of more than $1 million in false claims.[15] One study notes that as a result of such schemes, certain firms have been forced to raise their insurance rates by as much as 25 percent.[16] Sadly, these frauds could not be perpetrated if certain members of the legal and medical professions did not lend their assistance.[17]

A second type of fraud involves crimes by insurers against the insured. This may involve a handful of con men operating within one or more states, or a well-funded and organized group operating internationally. Not infrequently, it may include well-respected members of the industry who make false representations to the insured in order to stave off the financial collapse of their companies. This second category encompasses both shell and established firms.

Shell firms are numerous, and may involve members of organized crime. The felons will first establish a paper company, either within the United States or at off-shore locations. In the case of one such firm, the organizers employed more than 25 salesmen and falsified the company's balance sheets to reflect assets of $200 million in order to induce the public to buy insurance from their shell firm. The shell in this case was newly created, specifically with this fraud as its intent. In some instances, shells may be dormant companies that had lawful objectives at one time but fell into financial difficulties. Criminal elements will gain control of the shell and proceed to create false assets. After establishing the appearance of financial health and activity, the felons will begin to barrage both individuals and firms with literature and promotional material. The premiums paid by these unsuspecting policyholders are then funneled into other ventures or the pockets of these felons. When a policyholder files a legitimate claim, he is usually faced with numerous delays and will be told that reimbursement is imminent. If the claim is small, he may in fact be paid. However, if the claim is large, the felons will delay payment and finally disappear, leaving behind only an empty shell and numerous victims. Millions have been lost by the public as a result of these schemes.

Frauds are also perpetrated by management and usually have as their targets both the policyholders and stockholders. They may involve other companies, either in or out of the industry. In these frauds, management may in fact be looting the firm's assets. Loans and kickbacks are often made to outside associates in the form of consultant fees for nonexistent services.[18] One such case involved the now classic case of Equity Funding. Once considered the Cinderella of Wall Street, by 1972 the company included savings and loan associations, real estate, oil and gas ventures, and large investments in insurance. Since 1964, however, the firm had been falsifying its financial reports. It claimed to have more than $20 million in bonds with a Midwestern bank and to have loaned millions of dollars to mutual funds.

When the fraud was finally discovered, it was learned that there were no bonds, the loans to mutual funds were nonexistent, and more than 60 percent of the company's insurance policies were bogus.[19]

Equity Funding, some experts note, is only the tip of the iceberg.[20] A more recent case involving a large Pennsylvania insurance firm showed a similar pattern. The firm's insurance sales had increased from $325,000 to more than $57 million in a period of five years.[21] The company's stock had reached a price of more than $20 per share. It sold insurance to automobile owners in more than 20 states. Government investigators later learned that the firm had actually been broke, and that it had manipulated its assets to give the impression of increased earnings when severe losses were being incurred.

In a more recent case, more than 100,000 policyholders currently stand to lose money. The insurance firm, well-known in the Southern part of the United States, sold life insurance policies to many residents of its home state. The company had represented to its policyholders (many of whom are poor blacks) that it would pay the cash value of the policy on demand or provide a loan based on its value. Policyholders, however, learned later that the firm would not honor its commitments; and they were not aware of the company's poor financial condition. The firm's management had altered the company's records to give the appearance of financial growth, when in fact the firm was suffering setbacks. Although the state insurance agency knew of the firm's plight, little or no action was taken for more than a year. This case illustrates not only the ease with which management can rape an insurance firm, but also the laxity of controls in a multibillion dollar industry.

There are various clues that should alert investigators of insurance frauds, such as situations in which the same lawyers and doctors appear to be handling a large volume of injury claims. Cases in which the same individuals appear to be filing a large number of claims should also be a tip-off to the investigator. Firms with off-shore offices and exaggerated promises should also be suspect. Firms with brief business histories or that have been dormant for long periods of time may require further investigation, along with management that displays profits at a time when the insurance industry in general is weak. Unfortunately, the industry at present is regulated largely by state insurance commissions.[22] The federal investigative apparatus has little or no jurisdiction except when publicly held firms are involved.

This has led critics to assert that lax regulations and the very nature and legal framework of the insurance industry permit wide-scale frauds. It is claimed that many such frauds have been swept under the carpet by local politicians who control the state insurance agencies. In one Southern state, for example, federal investigators charged that the governor himself had intervened in the investigation of a possible insurance fraud and made its successful prosecution impossible.[23] There can be little doubt that if the wide-scale frauds in this industry are to be curtailed, a review of the entire industry is necessary. Further, a more effective regulatory and legal framework must be established. At present, both are lacking.

Notes

1. Ron Roach, "Arabs on Student Visas Charged in Fraudulent Insurance Claims," *Washington Post*, February 16, 1977, p. D-16; also, based on a number of interviews with security offices in the insurance industry, I drew the conclusion that insurance frauds are being perpetrated not only to fund the covers of criminals but also those of political extremist elements. For example, one insurance security official informed me that Palestinian Liberation Organization agents may have been involved in several West Coast insurance frauds.

2. Based on my interviews with people who are knowledgeable in the workings of the insurance industry; also based on interviews with prosecutors (both federal and local), as well as government investigators.

3. "Conviction in Fraudulent Fire Claims Scheme Obtained in Chicago," *National District Attorneys Association Economic Crime Digest* II (October 1975):169.

4. Mike Shanahan, "Union Officials Reportedly Feted in Insurance Deals," *Washington Post*, October 11, 1977, p. A-14; see also, Jack Anderson and Les Whitten, "Insurance Probe Eyes Kleindiest," *Washington Post*, September 27, 1977, p. B-13.

5. Robert E. Keeton, *Basic Text on Insurance Law* (St. Paul, Minn.: West, 1971), pp. 12, 20; also, for a review of insurance law, see William F. Young, Jr., *Cases and Materials on the Law of Insurance* (Mineola, N.Y.: Foundation Press, 1971).

6. William F. Young, Jr., *Cases and Material on the Law of Insurance*, p. 752.

7. For elaboration on the law of mutual funds, see Harry G. Henn, *Handbook of the Law of Corporations and Other Business Enterprises* (St. Paul, Minn.: West, 1970), pp. 608-610.

8. U.S. Congress, Committee on Government Operations, *Report on Institutional Investors' Common Stock—Holdings and Voting Rights* (Washington, D.C.: Government Printing Office, 1976), pp. 69-98.

9. *State ex. rel. Duffy Attorney General* v. *Western Auto Supply Company*, 134 Ohio St. 163 (1931).

10. "Eight Actors Convicted in Fraudulent Insurance Claim Ring," *National District Attorneys Association Economic Crime Digest* (November-December 1975):18.

11. Chamber of Commerce of the United States, *White Collar Crime* (Washington, D.C.: Chamber of Commerce of the United States, 1974), p. 6.

12. *United States* v. *Kenofskey*, 243 U.S. 440 (1917).

13. *United States* v. *Love*, 465 F.2d 408 (5th Cir., 1972).

14. "Insurance Claims," *National District Attorneys Association Economic Crime Digest* (December 1974):351.

15. Chamber of Commerce of the United States, *White Collar Crime*, p. 42.

16. Ibid., p. 43.

17. Ibid.

18. For a series of prosecutions in the area of insurance frauds, see *United States* v. *Hopps*, 331 F.2d 332 (4th Cir., 1964); *United States* v. *Brickey*, 426 F.2d 680 (8th Cir., 1970); *United States* v. *Wolfson*, 454 F.2d 60 (3rd Cir., 1972).

19. Raymond Dirks and Leonard Gross, *The Great Wall Street Scandal* (New York: McGraw-Hill, 1974); this book outlines one of the largest swindles in American history and certainly the largest in the insurance industry, the Great Equity Funding Fraud.

20. Philip Manuel, a well-known investigator and a staff member of the U.S. Senate Committee on Government Operations, with many years of experience in investigating insurance frauds, noted in correspondence with me that controls over the insurance industry are almost nonexistent, criminal elements take advantage of this situation, and defraud the public out of billions of dollars annually.

21. Bradley Graham, "SEC Charges a Broke Auto Insuror with Trying to Defraud Stockholders," *Washington Post*, August 19, 1977, p. D-6.

22. Jean Caper, "Insurance," *Washington Post*, October 2, 1977, pp. C-1, C-5.

23. "Louisiana Unit Delayed Insurance Case after Governor Intervened, SEC Charges," *Wall Street Journal*, May 23, 1977, p. 21.

10 Insider-Related Frauds

Embezzlement, pilferage, and other insider-related frauds cost the public more than $7 billion annually.[1] These crimes are not confined to any one class or group of individuals. They affect, and they are perpetrated by, people in all strata of society. A well-known New York attorney pleaded guilty in that state's Supreme Court to charges of embezzling funds from a large corporation.[2] In a separate case, the payroll clerk for an association for retarded children was charged with more than 70 counts of petty and grand larceny for allegedly stealing association funds for her personal use.[3] The clerk had falsified the association's business records. Not to be outdone, a $10,000 a year clerk in one of the large federal agencies was accused of stealing more than $800,000 from his employer.[4] The defendant had simply altered vouchers ordering payments to a large city for construction of a subway system.

Insider-related frauds involve the misuse of one's position in order to realize some monetary gain or privilege. They may also involve misuse for personal gain of confidential information acquired during the period of one's employment. The victim can be another individual, a firm, or a government agency that has placed the individual in a position of trust. This position is then misused to effect frauds in numerous industries and corporations; these, in turn, affect millions of consumers. However, for purposes of studying these frauds, we can place them in one or more of the following categories: (1) embezzlement, (2) pilferage-related thefts, and (3) dealings in confidential data.

Embezzlement

The conversion to one's own benefit of property or money belonging to another over which one has been given custody or over which one enjoys a fiduciary relationship is defined as being the crime of *embezzlement*. The victim may be a bank, an insurance company, or even an estate. Prosecutions for embezzlement are usually covered by local laws. However, if the mails are employed, or if interstate commerce is involved, then the felon can also be prosecuted under the federal bank statutes and mail fraud provisions. The former chairman of the board of a national retail chain of stores and three of his associates were charged by federal prosecutors with

85

siphoning off more than $2 million from the company.[5] In a separate case, a hospital administrator was prosecuted for embezzling more than $500,000 from his employer over a five-year period.[6] The elaborate fraud involved the laundering of hospital funds into more than a dozen bank accounts and the paying of firms that he controlled for nonexistent services and products.

Embezzlement is not a common-law crime; rather, it is the outgrowth of legislation enacted to combat an acknowledged problem. The earlier statutes made it a misdemeanor; but presently, it is a felony in most jurisdictions.[7] The statutes were passed to cover violations of trust perpetrated by clerks and others who had been given custody over money or property. This legislation reflected the growth of commerce and the need to ensure that those employees who were entrusted with valuables would not convert them to their own use. In the early nineteenth century, additional statutes were passed. These were designated to cover not only clerks, but also lawyers, bailees, trustees, and bankers who abused their positions of trust.[8]

The crime of embezzlement has five key elements: (1) a fraudulent intent, (2) a conversion, (3) of personal property, (4) belonging to another, and (5) by one in lawful possession. The absence of any one of these elements is a defense to the charge of embezzlement. In addition, although public officials also can commit the crime of embezzlement, many states, as well as the federal government, have enacted special legislation to address abuses of trust by their employees.

The primary element in embezzlement is the requisite *mens rea*, or fraudulent intent. There must be an intent to commit the act, to permanently deprive the rightful owner of his or her property. However, there are several defenses to a charge of embezzlement. The requisite intent can be shown to be lacking if the defendant can prove in court that in fact there was no intent to deprive the rightful owner of his money or property. For example, the defendant could claim that he actually intended to pay for the goods, and that these had been sold to him by the employer. It is also a valid defense if the defendant can show that he honestly believed that the property or money belonged to him and was, therefore, rightfully his. The defendant can also attempt to show that his capacity to form the requisite intent was lacking; for example, he may have been intoxicated, drugged, or suffering from amnesia. These can all serve to negate the fraudulent intent.[9]

There must be more than just a simple taking and carrying away, or a negligent taking. There must be a serious interference with the rightful owner's property rights. Further, the property must belong to another at the time of the crime. It must not be abandoned by the owner; he must still have lawful possession over it. A fortiori, one cannot be charged with embezzling one's own property; the converted property or money must belong to another. In addition, the embezzler must have taken possession over the property in a lawful manner. An unlawful taking and carrying away is larceny. The intent to defraud the rightful owner comes into play after the defendant has taken lawful custody over the property.

Members of a partnership can also be found guilty of embezzlement.[10] In one such case, New York prosecutors charged a partner in two large law firms with embezzling funds from those firms. The defendant had argued that since a partner has an interest in all partnership funds, he cannot be said to have taken what is his. The court noted that admittedly the defendant did have an interest in the partnership property; however, he had no right to take that share of the property which belonged to his other partners. A partner, like an employee, can thus be found guilty of embezzling the funds of another. The fact that one partner embezzles from another partner is itself irrelevant to the question of guilt.

Embezzlement is a serious crime; annual losses from this fraud exceed $1 billion.[11] Individual losses can be staggering; one European bank may have lost as much as $100 million from such a scheme. Three senior officials of the bank were eventually arrested.[12] Although detection of embezzlement has not been difficult previously, the growing use of computers for record-keeping purposes has begun to complicate this area significantly. Investigators should be wary of records that are not timely and appear "sloppy." Further, no one individual should have access and control over the entire disbursement process. Complaints, either from within or outside the firm, should be thoroughly investigated. They may be valid indications that something is wrong within the firm. Judges, too, must act decisively. In one recent District of Columbia case, the manager in charge of a firm's payroll embezzled more than $100,000 from his employer.[13] The judge fined him $1000 and suspended his sentence. This form of judicial behavior can hardly be said to discourage would-be embezzlers.

Pilferage-Related Thefts

Employee-related thefts exceed the $4 billion per year.[14] One study has put the figure even higher; it places these losses as high as $13 billion annually and notes that as many as 40 percent of all employees may be involved in employment-related thefts.[15] In some industries (e.g., cargo shipping), employee thefts have been known to account for as much as 80 percent of all industry losses.[16] A study of cargo facilities at major airports found that a majority of these losses were either the result of employees in collusion with fellow workers or with outside elements.[17] In a study of some 2000 cases, researchers found that more than $12 million worth of goods were lost as a result of employee theft or collusion.[18]

Employee thefts (pilferage) usually involve not only property and money but also time and services. In a number of cases, phony payrolls have been employed. The employee files false claims in which fictitious employees are added to the firm's payroll. Checks mailed to these individuals are later cashed by the operator of the scheme. No services, in turn, are performed for the company. Padding overtime records is also another form of employee fraud. Overtime payments are made either to the operator or to fictitious employees for what is represented as completed overtime work.

Employees have also been known to file false claims with their employer. These may involve claims for bogus business-related travel, a padding of expense accounts, or claims for nonexistent goods and services for which the employee seeks reimbursement. Credit-rating schemes are also common. Insiders within a particular firm may be involved: (1) in the sale of goods to customers known to be high risks, (2) in the falsification of applications for credit, or (3) in the creation of false credit accounts. The employee or employees may either be colluding with outsiders, or may in fact be the sole actor or actors in this fraud. Many such schemes have been uncovered in credit-related industries.

Pilferage-related frauds can also take simpler forms, such as a teller ringing up a $200 suit as a $100 sale or employees who steal over 100,000 pounds of lead by recasting it to fit their bodies. Such frauds may involve maintenance men who steal money from coin-operated vending machines or the theft of suits by an employee who falsifies records. These frauds are numerous and, at times, virtually impossible to prevent. Some firms have given up altogether and simply pass the cost on to the consuming public.

Prosecution at the local level usually comes under one of the larceny statutes. At the federal level, if use is made of the mails or if stolen goods are taken into interstate or foreign commerce, prosecution may be possible under an array of federal statutes. For purposes of larceny, however, six key elements must be proven by the prosecutors: (1) that there was a trespass, (2) a taking, (3) a carrying away, (4) of personal property, (5) of another, and (6) with intent to keep it. If the prosecution can show that the employee violated all six key elements, the latter can be successfully prosecuted for larceny.

The trespass requirement involves an unlawful interference with the employer's lawful possession of his property. The taking involves unauthorized control and dominion over the property in question. Property, under the common law, included only personal property. Modern statutes have broadened this to include goods severed from real property. The property in question, however, must belong to another individual; in case of an employee, to the employer. It must not be something that someone abandoned. Further, the employee must have the requisite intent to deprive his employer of the property.

Confidential Data-Related Frauds

An employer need not be defrauded exclusively of money or property for it to be a crime. He can be defrauded of valuable data or information or of the loyalty of his employees. For example, a large corporation was indicted for attempting to bribe the employee of another company into furnishing it with valuable trade secrets.[19] The court noted that part of the employer-employee relationship entailed an understanding that the employee would not wrongfully divulge confidential data to competitors of his employer.[20] Further, one who tampers with that relationship and attempts to induce an employee to betray his employer is attempting to defraud the latter of a lawful right.[21]

In a separate case, a firm that manufactures clinical laboratory instruments was approached by an individual who offered to sell it the plans for a new blood-counting device that had been developed by a competitor.[22] The new device had cost $1 million to develop and could bring in more than $100 million in sales for its developer within the next several years. The plans were valuable and could easily enhance the sales of a competitor. The police were called in on the case and, eventually, the theft was traced to an employee of the company that had developed this new blood-counting device. The case, however, was an exception to the norm. Few competitors would have turned down such an offer. Industrial espionage and the buying of confidential data is a multimillion dollar business, and employees play a vital role in this business.

Abuse of confidential data is not limited to the private sector. Government agencies and employees handle valuable trade secrets and confidential data regarding thousands of corporations daily. The data can be of great financial value for personal investment reasons or can be used simply for sale to competitors of the firm. However, at the federal level, the numerous agencies and boards have internal rules and regulations that provide for penalties for employees who misuse such confidential data. For example, Section 1905, Title 18, of the United States Code provides for fines of up to $1000 and/or imprisonment of up to one year for any federal official or employee who "divulges, discloses, or makes known in any manner or to any extent not authorized by law" any information that comes to him or her in the course of employment with the federal government. Other statutes provide for similar penalties for any federal employees who abuse or use for personal gain information of a confidential nature which they have gathered during the course of their employment.[23] A federal employee who divulges such confidential data can thus be prosecuted under federal law. Similar statutes are also found at the state level.[24]

Although it is illegal for employees to sell or divulge confidential data, prosecutions have been rare. Enforcement in this area has been and continues to be lax. In many instances, the firms themselves shy away from public exposure and will not bring charges against their employees. Their officials fear adverse publicity, for example, the fear that bankers or stockholders may lose confidence in a management that is lax in areas of security. Further, there is a large gray area, because many statutes are ambiguous or inconsistent or both. In addition, not all states have statutes that make it a crime to sell a firm's secret plans. Unless the mails are employed by the operator or interstate commerce is affected, the federal statutes will be of no value. Thus the criminal can avoid prosecution, and his employer will have civil recourse as the only alternative.

In many cases, theft of valuable data by employees can be curtailed if security measures are adequate. For example, the responsibilities of personnel should be rotated frequently. Internal checks should be conducted, and managers should be suspicious when employees live beyond their means. One federal employee who defrauded the government out of more than $500,000, bought 15 new cars; his supervisors took no notice. Duties should be segregated, and no one should have access to confidential data unless there is a "need to know." Although security measures can help, prosecution must be employed when needed. However, of greater importance is the development of a code of ethics that should be instilled in those who have access to confidential material. Insider-related frauds are a barometer of the ethical fiber of a society.

Notes

1. Chamber of Commerce of the United States, *White Collar Crime* (Washington, D.C.: Chamber of Commerce of the United States, 1974), p. 6.

2. "New York Lawyer Pleads in Massive Embezzlement," *National District Attorneys Association Economic Crime Digest* (March-April 1976):82.

3. "Nursing Home Study," *National District Attorneys Association Economic Crime Digest* (March-April-May 1975):17.

4. Timothy S. Robinson, "Court Frees Man Charged in Theft of $850,000," *Washington Post*, August 19, 1977, p. C-1.

5. "Head of Discount Chain Indicted for Embezzling," *Washington Post*, August 8, 1977, p. D-8.

6. Michael Weisskopf, "Brief, Lavish Fling of an Embezzler," *Washington Post*, September 24, 1977, p. B-1.

7. For a review of state statutes, see National Conference of States, *States Combat White Collar Crime* (Washington, D.C.: National Conference of State Legislatures, 1977), pp. 39-46.

8. For a review of the law of embezzlement, see Fred E. Inbau, James Thompson, and Claude R. Sowle, *Cases and Comments on Criminal Justice* (Mineola, N.Y.: Foundation Press, 1968), pp. 573-576.

9. For a review of defenses to the requisite *mens rea* in criminal cases, see ibid., pp. 645-720.

10. "New York Supreme Court Says Possible for Partner to Steal Partnership Funds," *National District Attorneys Association Economic Digest* (August-October 1975):172.

11. Chamber of Commerce of the United States, *White Collar Crime*, p. 6.

12. "Bank Probe Nets Three," *Washington Post*, April 26, 1977, p. D-8.

13. Laura A. Kiernan, "$1,000 Fine Is Levied in Embezzlement," *Washington Post*, November 15, 1977, p. C-3.

14. Chamber of Commerce of the United States, *White Collar Crime*, p. 6.

15. "$13 Billion Loss Estimate," *Security Digest* (November 2, 1977):7.

16. U.S. Department of Transportation, *Cargo Theft and Organized Crime* (Washington, D.C.: Government Printing Office, 1972), p. 9.

17. Ibid., p. 18.

18. Ibid.

19. *United States* v. *Proctor & Gamble*, 47 F.Supp.676 (1942).

20. Ibid., p. 678.

21. Ibid.

22. "How Technician Helped Trap a Spy," *Washington Post*, May 10, 1976, p. 53.

23. 18 U.S.C., sec. 1904, 1906, 1907, 1908, 1909.

24. For cases dealing with this area, see *Alexander* v. *United States*, 95 F.2d 873 (1938); and *United States* v. *Buckner*, 108 F.2d 921 (1940).

11 Antitrust and Restraint of Trade Practices

In the spring of 1974, the district attorney for Brooklyn, New York charged more than 50 private trash removal companies with restraining trade.[1] Nine officials of these firms were later indicted for perjury. Investigators for the district attorney had purchased a garbage truck and had entered the business posing as a small independent firm. They offered rates that were 30 percent lower than those of the other firms in the industry. Even with these lower rates, fewer than 1 percent of all area merchants signed up for their services. Prosecutors estimated that through a pattern of illegal trade practices, the trash removal companies had overcharged the merchants in the area some $20 million.

In late September 1977, six major Washington, D.C. real estate firms were convicted of violating provisions of the Sherman Antitrust Act.[2] The prosecutors charged that the defendants had agreed to raise and artificially maintain high rates, thus depriving the public of a free market.[3] The defendant firms faced possible fines of up to $1 million, and firm executives faced possible prison sentences of up to three years. The firms also faced civil suits from the private sector.

Antitrust and restraint-of-trades practices cost the American public billions of dollars in higher prices. Some experts place the figure well above the $20 billion mark, but no one is certain as to what the real costs are. Military officials have informed the U.S. Congress that illegal trade practices have inflated national security contracts to the point where the military is powerless to remedy the situation.[4] At the state level, one study has detailed how a handful of large supermarket chains have inflated retail meat prices while driving down the prices paid to livestock producers.[5] These practices are increasing both in frequency and in degree, and only concerted efforts will produce a constructive solution.

The Need for Free Competition

The theory behind a free marketplace is that if a society is allowed free competition, unrestrained by either government or the private sector, resources will be allocated in an optimal manner. Corporations will produce in accord with the needs of the marketplace, and consumers will have freedom of choice. If the firm meets the needs of the economic sector, then it will make

93

a profit. Theoretically, business and consumer will both profit from this free marketplace.

In a *monopolistic* environment, resources will not be employed in an optimal manner. The monopolist maximizes profits at the expenses of society by producing at the point where marginal revenue equals marginal cost. Society pays more for less. Barriers to the entry of other businessmen into the marketplace ensure the monopolist total control. These barriers may be artificial, for example, legislated by the state, or they may be created and maintained by the enormous resources and funds at the command of the monopolist.

Commerce may also be restrained by an *oligopoly*, a marketplace dominated by a small number of sellers. Although oligopoly may be preferred over monopoly, it too limits entry into the marketplace and gives a handful of large firms enormous leverage over the economy. A *monopsony* occurs when there is only one buyer, the opposite of a monopoly. For example, it may be state authorized, as where the state has legislated that all iron ore will be sold to the state-owned corporation.

There are also instances of an *oligopsony*. This situation involves a marketplace dominated by a small number of large buyers. In European countries and in the international arena, the cartel has made its presence felt for many years. This entity is usually composed of a small number of firms that set an agreed price and limit production to agreed quantities. In a recent antitrust suit, the U.S. Justice Department charged two large firms with having conspired to set agreed prices in the giant turbine industry.[6] The two companies dominated 90 percent of the industry.

Combinations to restrain trade are not new. They existed in the days of ancient Rome, and the common-law jurists made many references to them. The East India companies of the Middle Ages were prime examples of this. These combinations generally take the form of agreements to fix the price and limit the freedom of competition in the marketplace. They touch the business world as well as the professions, the objective being to benefit the conspirators at the expense of the public. The schemes are usually elaborate and very subtle. The federal government has charged, for example, the funeral home industry with restraints of trade through such subtle practices.[7] The airport car-rental industry has also come under scrutiny. The government is concerned that airport contracts in the car-rental industry tend to limit competition and fix prices.[8]

Under the early common law, agreements that fixed prices were illegal. The kings of England were concerned that such agreements would limit their revenues and, as a result, restraints of trade were made criminal. Businessmen who attempted to corner the marketplace were tried under the conspiracy laws, and contracts that had as their objective the restraint of trade were void per se. The church also frowned on these practices. There was serious concern that monopolistic practices could limit the powers of the crown and simultaneously increase the number of poor people.

With the advent of the Renaissance, large banking facilities rose to power. Trade increased dramatically, and multinational firms made their appearance. Kings relied heavily for war supplies on the powerful business interests. The feudal levies had given way to professional armies, and the Medicis and their counterparts made funds available for these armies. In return, they were able to obtain certain business concessions; combinations that sought to regulate business and fix prices were no longer unlawful per se. Large and powerful guilds had made their appearances in many European towns. Their powers were immense, and the authorities generally tolerated them. A new legal approach was developed—an accommodation to the political realities of Renaissance Europe. Monopolies were tolerated, provided they served some legitimate purpose. In 1613 the now classic case of *Rogers* v. *Parrey* was decided.[9] The court held that contracts in restraint of commerce were not unlawful, provided that: (1) the restraint was reasonable, (2) partial, and (3) supported by consideration. Combinations were tolerated if they served some legitimate objective, and if they were limited in time and geography.

In the United States, until passage of the Sherman Act in 1890, two schools of thought dominated the legal arena. One view adhered to the earlier common law and held that all agreements that aimed at limiting competition were illegal per se. A second view held that such agreements should be upheld, provided they were reasonable and of some benefit to society. In the early 1870s, however, pressure was placed on Congress to pass legislation in this area.[10] After the American Civil War, vast economic concentrations began to take shape. In the forefront were the railroads. The National Anti-Monopoly Cheap Freight Railway League was formed by the small business interests to combat the powerful railroad conglomerates.[11] A suspicion of big business was deeply rooted in the American fiber.[12] As a result, other groups sprang up, such as the National Grange and the National Farmers Alliance.[13] In the 1880s, Congress began to pay attention, as a result of the growing and increasingly vocal reform groups. In 1887 the Interstate Commerce Act was enacted, which outlawed some of the discriminatory practices of the railroad giants. Three years later, the first of the federal antitrust laws was enacted. A new era began.

The Federal Antitrust Laws

The first of these federal statutes was the Sherman Act. Section 1 of the act makes all contracts, combinations, and conspiracies in restraint of trade in either interstate or foreign commerce illegal. Any combination or agreement between competitors, formed for the purpose of fixing prices, is illegal, provided it affects interstate or foreign commerce. In one of the earlier U.S. Supreme Court cases on the matter, some of the large oil firms, facing a large supply of gasoline, agreed to purchase surplus gasoline from the independent refiners who had no storage facilities.[14] The large firms intended to store their own gasoline for the day when prices would increase as supply diminished. The action was held as violating Section 1 of the act.

A common problem in antitrust cases is the meaning of *price fixing* under the Sherman Act. The courts have traditionally given it a broad definition. In one case, an agreement between competitors on how much they will produce was viewed as price fixing. Conversely, an agreement among buyers as to the price they will pay was also held to be price fixing. There are some exceptions to this broad definition, and these will be discussed later in the chapter. Within the class of exempt organizations, however, are businesses that are heavily regulated by the federal government; for example, airlines are regulated by the Civil Aeronautics Board (CAB), and their price structure is not in violation of the act.

It is generally illegal for a firm to fix the price of its product by contract. There are exceptions, for example, when authorized by state fair laws. In 1937 Congress passed legislation that exempted certain types of resale price-maintenance agreements, provided they were valid under the laws of their own states.[15] If a state does not have fair trade laws, then a resale agreement is in violation of Section 1 of the Sherman Act. Attempts to set a minimum or maximum price on a product, unless there is state legislation that governs that sale, will be in violation of the act.[16]

Among companies engaged in the same business or manufacturing the same products, an agreement to divide up the market is illegal;[17] such an agreement would give each firm an effective monopoly over a segment of that market.[18] Any attempted restriction by the seller of a buyer's right to resell may be a violation of Section 1. Attempts to fix the resale price would also be illegal. The theory behind this is that once a manufacturer sells his product to a buyer or buyers, it is no longer his, and he thus has no right to place any restrictions on the movement of that product or the actions of the buyer. Restrictions pertaining to the territory within which a buyer may resell his products are also illegal. The intent behind Section 1 is to maintain a free and competitive marketplace; any restrictions on that freedom could be illegal.

Section 3 of the Sherman Act makes the provisions of Section 1 applicable to the District of Columbia and to all U.S. territories. Section 2 of the act prohibits monopolies or attempts to establish a monopoly over any area of interstate or foreign commerce. It includes any conspiracies or combinations to monopolize any area of interstate or foreign commerce. Section 2, however, does not outlaw monopolies per se; something more than just a monopoly is required to make it a violation of this section.

If monopolists use predatory or coercive tools to gain control of a market, a Section 2 violation could be found. However, there must be a willful act to gain control or maintain control over a sector of the marketplace in order to sustain such a finding.[19] For example, there is every reason to believe that organized crime figures who employ coercive tactics to gain control over a sector of the marketplace could easily be prosecuted under the Sherman Act. Despite this, the government has made little, if any, use of the act in this area. To reiterate, there must be a willful act plus a monopoly over a sector of the marketplace to make it a Section 2 violation.

The second issue of major importance in antitrust cases concerns monopolistic control. This will vary from case to case. Obviously, a firm that controls 90 percent of a market can be said to have the requisite monopolistic power over that sector of the economy. In one case, the U.S. Supreme Court held that 20 percent control over an area of the marketplace may not be sufficient.[20] There have been other cases in which lower courts have differed in what they considered to be the requisite market power. For example, one court has noted that 60 percent control was sufficient, while another court held that 75 percent was sufficient. Much depends on the facts of the case, the market itself, and the product involved.

Attempts to monopolize a market are also in violation of Section 2. The fact that the attempt has failed does not exempt it from prosecution under the Sherman Act.[21] The test is whether the means employed, if successful, would have been sufficient to bring about monopoly control. The prosecutors, however, must show (as in the case with other categories of crime) the requisite intent.[22] Not infrequently, such proof is difficult to establish. The means employed must be unfair, as measured by the standards of acceptable business practice. For example, discriminatory pricing, boycotts, and refusal to deal with a smaller business can be regarded as unfair methods.

In late December 1973, a federal grand jury in Pittsburgh, Pennsylvania brought an indictment against six large manufacturers of construction material.[23] The defendants were charged with conspiring to fix prices, in violation of the Sherman Antitrust Act. This was the latest in a series of prosecutions of antitrust cases that began with the landmark case of 1961. That first major antitrust prosecution involved the heavy electrical equipment industry. Chief among the defendants were several vice presidents of the General Electric and Westinghouse Electric corporations.[24] The probe had begun in 1959, after the federal prosecutors were informed that buyers were receiving identical bids from the manufacturers of heavy electrical equipment. The government later charged that the defendants, through a series of secret meetings and negotiations, had fixed prices and divided up the market. Almost all the defendants entered pleas of guilty. The case set a major precedent; dozens of business executives received prison sentences and minor fines. It signified that at least some courts were willing to apply the sanctions of the Sherman Act. Critics charge, however, that those sanctions have been applied too leniently. In the later case, the maximum prison sentence received did not exceed 30 days.

In 1914 Congress enacted the Clayton Act, key provisions of which are Sections 3, 4, 6, and 7. Section 3 makes it unlawful to lease or make a sale of commodities, or fix a price therefor, on condition or agreement that the lessee or purchaser will not use or deal in the commodities of a competitor of the seller or lessor.[25] The section seeks to curb behavior that will decrease competition or create a monopoly, but applies only to commodities and not services or real property. These market products are covered by the Sherman Act.

Additionally, tie-in arrangements are in violation of the section if their objective or outcome is to lessen competition. For example, if a seller informs a buyer that he will not sell him product X unless the buyer also buys product Y, the seller is in violation if the net outcome lessens competition. The seller is making the sale of X conditional on the purchase of Y, obviously with the intent of creating a monopoly. This must be proven. However, there are exceptions to this, such as where the seller has a patent to a product and enjoys a legitimate monopoly in that area. If he attempts to extend his monopoly into the nonpatented area, though, he may be in violation of Section 3. The tie-in arrangement, if it lessens competition, is illegal.

Section 4 of the act provides that any individual who is injured in his business or property by another who has violated the antitrust laws can sue and recover "threefold the damages by him sustained, the cost of the suit, including reasonable attorney's fee."[26] The U.S. Supreme Court has held that the purpose of the antitrust laws is best served if private parties are allowed to bring private litigation.[27] For purposes of this section, *business* may include an injured party's commercial or industrial enterprise as well as his employment or occupation.[28] States and localities can also qualify as plaintiffs under this section if they can show injury to their business or property. The intent of this section is to enlarge the policing sphere of the antitrust laws by allowing both private and local political bodies the power to sue violators.[29]

Section 6 exempts agricultural groups and labor unions from prosecution under the Sherman and Clayton Acts. Agricultural groups instituted for self-help and not conducted for profit are not subject to the antitrust laws; the Capper-Volstead Act extends this exemption to agricultural cooperatives.[30] However, the exemption does not apply to coercive actions, such as boycotts. Nevertheless, the Secretary of the U.S. Department of Agriculture can take action if the cooperative is engaged in restraint of trade.[31] In a recent case, a Federal Trade Commission (FTC) administrative law judge held that a California cooperative should be disbanded because it was not exempt under the Capper-Volstead Act.[32] The cooperative had exchanged marketing information with other similar groups. The FTC, however, dismissed the case, holding that the cooperative was exempt from prosecution under the antitrust laws.

Labor unions are also exempt from prosecution under the antitrust laws. However, there are limitations to this exemption. Unions engaged in pursuit of the interest of their members are generally exempt, but the union cannot assist nonlabor groups in establishing control over a marketplace. The test is whether the activity and agreements a labor union participates in are aimed at promoting the legitimate interests of its members. For example, unions can enter into agreements that impose minimum wages or fixed working hours. These are legitimate and accepted objectives of a labor union and are not proscribed by the antitrust laws.

Section 7, when originally enacted in 1914, prohibited firms engaged in interstate or foreign commerce from acquiring stock in a firm also engaged in interstate or foreign commerce where the effect of such an acquisition would be to lessen competition. This section, however, did not cover acquisitions affected by purchase of the assets of another firm. In 1950 Section 7 was amended to include acquisitions affected by the purchase of the assets of another firm. (This amendment was a result of the passage of the Celler-Kefauver Act.)[33] The intent of this section is to prevent anticompetitive behavior before it occurs. In a recent case, a New Jersey-based steel firm had begun to acquire stock in another steel firm.[34] The New Jersey-based firm admitted that it had purchased 5 percent of the stock in the other company and expressed concern about possible antitrust implications. The wide-ranging effect of Section 7 proscriptions has apparently created a corporate-level awareness of possible antitrust activity.

In 1914 Congress enacted the Federal Trade Commission Act. The key provisions of that act are Sections 5(a)(1) and 5(a)(3). The act makes unfair methods of competition illegal and seeks to curb unfair or deceptive practices. It gives the FTC exclusive enforcement powers and allows the localities to pass their own fair trade laws. The great majority of our states have since enacted such legislation.[35] Section 5 authorizes the FTC to take action to stop activity that is in violation of the antitrust laws; it grants the agency prosecutorial powers in this arena. The FTC can go to a federal court and obtain a cease-and-desist order, which is a civil remedy; criminal matters must be referred by the FTC to the Justice Department for prosecution.

In 1936 Congress enacted the Robinson-Patman Act as an amendment to Section 2 of the Clayton Act. The objective of the 1936 amendment was to prevent sellers from discriminating in the pricing of their products.[36]

Under the Robinson-Patman Act (Section 2(a) of the Clayton Act), it is illegal to discriminate in price between various buyers. Additionally, though, the product sold to these different buyers must be of similar quality and type, and the outcome must affect competition. The seller, by offering a favorable price to a select buyer, injures other buyers and prevents a free market. As a result, both the seller and buyer can be guilty of a violation of the act.[37] Services and intangibles are not covered, however, and price discrimination in this are is not a violation. Nevertheless, a violation of the other antitrust laws may be charged. Ultimately, the intent of the act is to maintain prices at a competitive level and free of manipulation and interference by nonmarket forces.

Although the objective of the act is to maintain a competitive marketplace, there are several exceptions; for example, the Webb-Pomerence Act provides that American firms joined together for export purposes are immune from prosecution under the antitrust laws. Other statutes, such as the Magnuson-Moss Act, the Fair Credit Opportunity Act, and the Fair Packing Act, are also aimed at protecting the consumer from predatory and monopolistic behavior.

Exemptions to the Antitrust Laws

The antitrust laws, although broad and sweeping in appearance, contain numerous loopholes; large sectors of our economy are not covered by them, and jurisdiction has been allocated to a variety of agencies under numerous statutes enacted by Congress. In addition to the exemptions provided under the state fair trade laws, labor unions, agricultural cooperatives, and stock exchanges registered with the federal government are exempt. The Securities Exchange Act of 1934 permits the brokerage industry to set fixed commission rates that apply to all member firms of the exchange.

Bank mergers are specifically exempt from antitrust laws. The Attorney General of the United States may challenge such a merger in court, but not as a violation of the antitrust laws. Railroads, motor transport carriers, and interstate water carriers are also exempt from prosecution under the antitrust laws. The Interstate Commerce Commission (ICC) has been delegated the authority to regulate and police these sectors of the economy. Agreements on prices, traffic, mergers, and revenues must be approved by the ICC, which is not bound by the antitrust laws. Individuals injured by these practices have recourse to the ICC.

The antitrust laws have limited application in the insurance industry. They apply only if states have not enacted legislation in this area. Conversely, state laws regulating the insurance industry have curtailed the enforcement of antitrust laws. However, coercive acts can bring the Sherman Act into play. In the airline industry, the Federal Aviation Act has supplanted the antitrust laws. The Civil Aeronautics Board (CAB) has been authorized to police and regulate that industry. Unfair or deceptive practices, as well as noncompetitive behavior, fall under the policing authority of the CAB. This large and important economic area has been taken out of the realm of the antitrust laws.

Policing the Antitrust Laws

Enforcement of the antitrust legislation lies with four entities: (1) the private individual, under Section 4 of the Clayton Act, (2) the states, (3) the FTC, and (4) the Justice Department. The success of these laws rests heavily on the ability and integrity of the enforcers. In great part, the laxity of enforcement of these laws has been due to the lack of activity by the enforcers.

Admittedly, the private sector is limited in its policing capability. Few small businesses or individuals have the necessary resources to fund extensive and prolonged litigation. The states are also handicapped by limited resources.[38] For example, a study of 53 jurisdictions across the country found that only 43 have any prosecutors assigned to do antitrust work;[39] only 24 of these offices employ full-time attorneys in this area;[40] and the majority of these offices employ only three antitrust attorneys.[41] The state prosecutors are seriously handicapped in every respect. Only 6 states allocate more than $200,000 to their antitrust units;[42] only 10 states have budgets in the area of $100,000 to $200,000 allocated to antitrust units;[43] and more than 12 states have budgets of less than $100,000.[44]

In 1973 the state of New Jersey charged more than 12 national firms and over 100 local firms with violations of the antitrust laws.[45] The state charged that the defendants had engaged in a pattern of preferential treatment and had made kickbacks to local political figures. Through a series of complex schemes, the defendants had limited competition and had dominated the market. The suit asked for more than $500 million in damages; the litigation proved costly and time consuming. New Jersey, however, is a large state with a sizable prosecutorial staff. Many smaller states, with limited staffs and small budgets, can hardly engage in time-consuming and expensive litigation. Antitrust cases, unfortunately, require large commitments in terms of both resources and manpower. Few states can afford that luxury.

To reiterate, the FTC has been delegated the authority to police the antitrust area. However, the agency suffers from excessive red tape and has no criminal jurisdiction; it can only refer cases to the Justice Department for criminal action. The FTC does have administrative and civil jurisdiction. It can file a complaint against a violator in a federal court, but the only remedy is a cease-and-desist order. Essentially, the Commission can only attempt to prohibit future behavior and can do little about the past. Administrative trials held within the FTC are the other option available to the agency. However, these administrative proceedings are lengthy, complicated, and civil rather than criminal in nature. Further, a defendant can delay the outcome through an elaborate route of appeals. Some FTC cases have been known to take many years before reaching a conclusion. Needless to say, the deterrent impact has been softened substantially.

The Justice Department's Antitrust Division is charged with the criminal (and often civil) prosecution of antitrust violations. However, the Justice Department depends on the FTC and other agencies to investigate complex cases, which are then referred to its Antitrust Division. Although the Department has indicated it will employ the Federal Bureau of Investigation (FBI) in the investigation of antitrust violations, critics note that the FBI has no expertise in this area and may take many years before it develops that capability. At present, the Antitrust Division depends largely on the regulatory agencies for criminal referrals in this area. Since many agency cases, including those of the FTC, are handled either administratively or through the consent-decree route, most never reach the division.

The division itself has been lax in prosecuting antitrust violations. In 1968, for example, the division filed 16 criminal cases involving price fixing; in 1970, with a larger staff and budget, the division brought only 4 cases; by 1975, under public pressure, prosecutions rose to 29 cases.[46] The division has fared no better in the area of monopolies: in 1968 it brought no prosecutions; in 1975 it brought 5.[47] This is hardly an impressive record for a unit with a budget of over \$20 million annually.[48] The FTC employs 200 attorneys in its antitrust section (the Bureau of Competition).[49] The record of both these agencies in the area of antitrust enforcement has been extremely poor.

The legal armament exists; large sums of money have been allocated to the federal apparatus to combat antitrust and restraint of trade practices. Admittedly, the local prosecutorial offices lack the necessary expertise and resources to do battle in this area. In the private sector, few individuals can afford prolonged and complex civil litigation. Many antitrust cases require well-trained investigators and lawyers who must piece together complex financial conspiracies. By necessity, the federal apparatus must bear the greater brunt of this battle. To date, it has not. Without adequate enforcement of our antitrust laws, we may soon find that our free enterprise system may become a thing of the past. We may also find ourselves serving a handful of multinational corporations and their managerial masters. The stakes are too great.

Notes

1. Public Citizen Staff Report, *White Collar Crime* (Washington, D.C.: Congress Watch, 1974), p. 17.

2. Nancy L. Ross, "Six Realty Firms Are Convicted of Fee Conspiracy," *Washington Post*, September 29, 1977, pp. A-1, A-6.

3. Ibid., p. A-6. See also, for a background to the history of the Sherman Antitrust Act, Attorney General's National Committee to Study Antitrust Laws, *Antitrust Developments* (Chicago, Ill.: American Bar Association, 1968), pp. 1-39.

4. "Rickover Asks Hill Help on Shipbuilders Claims," *Washington Post*, March 25, 1977, p. A-9.

5. Lou Cannon, "Big Food Chains Control Meat Prices, Study Says," *Washington Post*, July 31, 1977, p. A-7.

6. Jack Anderson and Les Whitten, "Antitrust Chief and Big Business," *Washington Post*, February 7, 1977, p. C-23.

7. "Stiffer State Measures for Funeral Homes Urged by Aide; FTC Efforts Endorsed," *Wall Street Journal*, August 17, 1977, p. 2.

8. Carole Shifrin, "FTC Begins Investigation of Airport Rental Space," *Washington Post*, May 25, 1977, p. D-1.

9. 80 Eng. Rep., 1012 (1613).

10. A.D. Neale, *The Antitrust Laws of the U.S. of America* (Cambridge, England: Univ. Press, 1970), pp. 11, 12.

11. Ibid., p. 12.

12. Ibid.

13. Ibid.

14. *United States* v. *Socony Vacum Oil Company*, 310 U.S. 150 (1940).

15. 15 U.S.C., 1.

16. A.D. Neale, *The Antitrust Laws of the U.S. of America*, pp. 32-51.

17. Ibid., pp. 32, 33.

18. *Timken Roller Bearing Company* v. *United States*, 341 U.S. 593 (1951).

19. *American Tobacco Company* v. *United States*, 328 U.S. 781 (1946).

20. *The Cellophane Case*, 351 U.S. 377 (1956).

21. *American Tobacco Company* v. *United States*, 328 U.S. 781 (1946).

22. *Times-Picayune* v. *United States*, 345 U.S. 594 (1952); see also, Attorney General's National Committee to Study Antitrust Laws, *Antitrust Developments*, p. 34.

23. Public Citizens Staff Report, *White Collar Crime*, pp. 16, 17.

24. Marshall Clinard and Richard Quinney, eds., *Criminal Behavior Systems* (New York: Holt, Rinehart and Winston, 1967), pp. 139-145.

25. See A.D. Neale, *The Antitrust Laws of the U.S. of America*, pp. 203-219, for a discussion of Section 3 of the Sherman Act.

26. 15 U.S.C.A., sec. 15.

27. *Perma-Life Mufflers, Inc., et al.* v. *International Parts Corporation, et al.*, 382 U.S. 134, 139 (1968).

28. See *Image & Sound Service Corporation* v. *Altec Service Corporation*, 148 F.Supp. 237 (D.Mass. 1956); and also *Vines* v. *General Outdoor Advertising Company*, 171 F.2d 487 (2d Cir., 1948).

29. For an indepth review of consumer litigation involving the antitrust laws, see Milton Handler and Michael D. Blechman, "Antitrust and the Consumer Interest: the Fallacy of *Parens Patriae* and a Suggested New Approach," *Yale L.J.* 85 (1976): 624.

30. 7 U.S.C., sec. 291.

31. Ibid., sec. 292.

32. "Lettuce Co-op Wins Dismissal by FTC of Price-Fix Charge," *Wall Street Journal*, August 8, 1977, p. 17.

33. Attorney General's National Committee to Study Antitrust Laws, *Antitrust Development*, p. 65.

34. "Antitrust Problems Seen by Washington Steel in Combine," *Wall Street Journal*, August 17, 1977, p. 9.

35. Criminal Justice and Consumer Affairs Staff, *The States Combat White Collar Crime* (Washington, D.C.: National Conference of State Legislatures, 1976), pp. 46-51.

36. A.D. Neale, *The Antitrust Laws of the U.S. of America*, pp. 225-229.

37. *Federal Trade Commission* v. *Fred Meyer, Incorporated*, 390 U.S. 341 (1968).

38. National Association of Attorneys General, *Selected Statistics on the Office of Attorney General* (Raleigh, N.C.: National Association of Attorneys General, 1975), p. 67.

39. Ibid.

40. Ibid.

41. Ibid.

42. Ibid.

43. Ibid.

44. Ibid.

45. Public Citizens Staff Report, *White Collar Crime*, p.17.

46. U.S. Department of Justice, *Annual Report of the Attorney General of the United States for 1975* (Washington, D.C.: Government Printing Office, 1976), p. 116.

47. Ibid.

48. Timithy D. Schellhardt, "Merger of Antitrust Division, FTC Unit is Ordered for Study by Attorney General," *Wall Street Journal*, April 11, 1974, p. 4.

49. Ibid.

12 Crime by Computer

Several years ago, the district attorney for Nassau County, Long Island, New York announced the arrest of the former supervisor of accounts receivable for a large national insurance company on charges of embezzling more than $20,000 from the firm.[1] According to the prosecutors, the defendant had put false vouchers through the firm's main computer. The computer, in turn, had issued checks made out to a fictitious firm controlled by the defendant. The fraud was uncovered when one of the company's clerks noticed that one of the refund checks being mailed to the defendant's fictitious firm was much larger than the usual refund payment.

In August 1977, officials at a large Northeastern university uncovered a scheme involving payments by students who wanted their grades altered in the school's computer center.[2] The investigation was sparked by a series of letters to university officials that outlined the scheme and the individuals involved. The investigators found that several thousand dollars had been paid to a university employee who made changes on grade cards that were later used to make entries in the university's computer. Although no one was prosecuted in the case, several students were expelled.

In another case, two women pleaded guilty in the theft of more than $400,000 from a union fund.[3] One of the two women had been employed by a corporation that handled the union's pension fund. The employee diverted funds to her accomplice from the union's pension fund by simply filling out false claim benefits and entering those into the company's computer. From 1967 through 1975, more than 600 checks were issued by the computer to the employee's accomplice.

These cases serve to illustrate a growing problem in the area of white-collar crime—crime by computer technology. With the assistance of this new technology, felons have netted vast fortunes. For example, while the average bank robbery realizes only about $15,000, the average computer theft nets about $400,000.[4] Some losses have passed the million dollar mark;[5] other cases, such as the Equity Funding fraud, have run into the billions of dollars. Experts estimate that the likelihood of such a crime being discovered by the authorities is one out of a hundred. One recent study places the annual loss at over $100 million, and this estimate does not involve the cost of investigating and prosecuting these crimes.[6] The problem is serious and increasing rapidly. Part of the problem is due to the failure of law enforcement to meet the challenges of the new and growing technology.

The mystique of the computer presents additional difficulties to criminal justice officials. However, regardless of the reasons for failure, there is a need to understand the computer felon and to develop a strategy to combat this new criminal challenge.

Categories of Computer Crime

With the rise of computer technology, traditional crime may become a thing of the past. Even sophisticated forms of white-collar crime have begun to show the influence of this new technology. For example, a complicated securities fraud was made possible, in part, because of the use of computer technology. From 1967 through 1973, a large national insurance company reported that its sales had increased by more than $50 million.[7] The fraud was made possible by use of a computer program code named *clean*, whereby the company's computer was programmed to freeze liabilities.[8] In an effort to increase earnings, more than $1 million in liabilities were hidden from the stockholders of the firm. The company's former president and founder, as well as its former chairman of the board, knew of the fraud.[9]

Computer crimes usually fall into one or more of five key categories. One of the more common, and often easiest to detect, is that of vandalism. This usually involves some form of damage to the computer itself or components of its system. The objective of this crime is to destroy either the system entirely, and thus make it inoperable, or to cause additional expense and delay to the user. These attacks may come from various sources. For example, labor-management disputes may give rise to vandalism; competitors may sabotage a computer system so as to undermine the financial stability of a firm; foreign agents may attack a computer for political objectives, especially where political extremist groups are involved. In one case, someone removed all the labels from 1500 reels of computer tape, which cost the firm large expenditures in both time and money in reidentifying the data.[10]

Another common form of computer crime involves valuable data—theft of information. Such crimes usually involve the theft of valuable computer programs and are usually committed by company insiders who have access to the firm's computer system and who can copy or take such programs for sale to competitors of the firm. Time-sharing situations have also come under criminal attack.

Use of computers for personal benefit—theft of services—is a growing problem. At present, both the governmental and private computer sectors have been victimized. There have been instances in which local politicians have used a municipality's computer for direct-mailing purposes in order to advance their political campaigns.[11] Criminal elements have been known to employ a university's computer system to advance their criminal objectives; and government employees have been known to use government computers to conduct their own private businesses.

Computers also enable criminals to steal large volumes of merchandise or other property by simple manipulation. Through access to a company's computer, criminals can place large orders and instruct the computer to have the merchandise delivered to specific locations. As an example of this, a large California-based telephone company was taken for more than a million dollars worth of merchandise by simple manipulation of its computer.[12] These crimes are listed as thefts of property. Burglary, in the computer age, will take on added dimensions.

The greatest threat from computer crime comes in the financial arena. Here, by simple manipulation of a computer system, fictitious assets and earnings can be created at the push of a button. In the Equity Funding case, top management officials began to falsify large numbers of insurance policies in late 1969.[13] Out of 97,000 policies, more than 60,000 were fictitious. These phony policies were assigned a secret code: "Department 99." The "99" designation enabled the computer billing programs to skip these bogus policies when bills were sent to policyholders. At audit time, when documentation on policies was requested by government investigators, the firm's officers stalled for time by simply saying the files were not immediately available.[14] They then used this extra time to forge the hard-copy files, which contained such things as health reports, contracts, etc. By the next day, they would have manufactured the policies that the investigators requested. The whole matter came to the surface only when a discharged official blew the whistle. The fraud cost the investors more than $1 billion in losses.[15] This was an example of a financial crime through the use of computers. These frauds are easiest to commit in a system where the computer is employed in financial processing, including payrolls, accounts payable and receivable, and storage and maintenance of files and financial data.[16]

Why Computers Are Easily Victimized

Computer technology has advanced beyond the ability of the average citizen to comprehend. Computers have grown in storage capacity and complexity.[17] The IBM 370 has a storage capacity of 7000 times that of the UNIVAC I, the first commercial computer. A standard reel of magnetic computer tape can hold over 30 million characters of information.[18] However, although computers have grown in complexity, their operation remains simple and vulnerable to criminal manipulation.

The first and most important stage in the computer operation is the input phase. During this stage, data is translated into a language that is intelligible to the computer.[19] Felons with access to this phase of the computer operation can manipulate the system by simply introducing false data into the computer.

They can also alter data and remove key input documents.[20] False accounts and credits can be easily fabricated at this stage. As an example, an officer of a large manufacturing firm fed the firm's computer false data, thus creating fictitious suppliers. The computer then ordered payments to be made to these accounts. In a period of less than two years, the felon defrauded his company of more than $1 million.[21]

The next key phase in a computer operation is the programming. During this stage, the computer is supplied with a logical sequence of step-by-step operations for the solution of problems.[22] Programs, however, can be stolen, altered, or even held for ransom. Several years ago, bandits robbed the Bank of America's Los Angeles branch and took with them several computer reels.[23] Realizing the value of the reels, they demanded a ransom. In another case, a major book publisher accused several of its employees of copying several million names from the firm's computer file and selling them to a competitor.[24] Programs can easily become the target of political extremist groups, as well as foreign intelligence agencies.

The third stage in a computer operation is the CPU, or central processing unit. This is the computer's nervous system—its brain. It directs the computer's operations. The CPU could easily become the target of a firm's competitors, as well as criminal elements. The destruction of the CPU would essentially cripple the operations of a firm that has computerized the bulk of its paper work. It is estimated that a firm with more than 90 percent of its records computerized would lose its viability after the destruction of the CPU.[25] An industrial society, heavily dependent on computerized record keeping, could find itself in great difficulty if key CPUs were destroyed.[26] Some experts estimate that the destruction of 100 key computer centers in this country could cripple the national economy. The CPU poses a tempting and easy target for determined criminal elements.

The fourth key stage is the output phase. During this stage, data is received from the CPU and translated into an intelligible language. Crimes involving this phase of a computer's operation usually involve thefts of valuable data.[27] Output data could easily be stolen and find its way into the growing black market. Military and industrial secrets would prove tempting prizes. Mr. Philip Manuel, a U.S. Senate investigator who has studied the problem of computer security for several years, notes that more than 90 percent of all computers in the public and private sectors are vulnerable to attack.

The last stage in the computer operation is the communication phase, which involves the use of telephone circuits to transmit data back and forth between computer systems and remote terminals. This stage is open to electronic penetration. Valuable data can be intercepted or altered. As an example of this, a felon gained access to a credit bureau's computer through the simple use of a telephone. Once having penetrated the system, he copied data from the files of the firm's clients.

Electronic penetration of the communication phase can take on several forms. The most common is that of wiretapping. A tap is directly connected to the telephone lines used to transmit the data from one computer system to another, or to a remote terminal. Messages are intercepted and recorded. Browsing is another form of penetration. This involves the tapping of an unauthorized terminal to a computer system. The felon, however, can gain access only if the system does not authenticate terminal entry. Electromagnetic pickup, yet another method of penetration, involves the interception of the radiation generated by a computer system.

Securing the Computer

Numerous security measures have been suggested for safeguarding the computer system from criminal attack. Some experts suggest that the system itself be kept under guard and be isolated from the other divisions of a firm.[28] It is suggested, further, that the programmer not operate the computer. In addition, experts note that no employee should have access for too long a period of time to any one stage of the computer's operation. Access shoud be on a need-to-know basis only.

However, a computer can be safeguarded but never made fully impregnable. The primary factor behind computerization has been the economic motive. Extreme security measures could easily nullify the economic feasibility of a computer system. Corporations are reluctant to turn their computer operations into armed camps. Security measures alone are not enough. There is a need for deterrence, which only law enforcement and prosecution can provide. However, at present, our investigatory and prosecutorial machinery has been slow to adapt to this new form of crime.[29] Our legal system has fallen behind our technology.

The Problem of Prosecution

The prosecution of computer crimes will involve the use of computer-generated evidence. Some legal experts take the position that our present rules of evidence can meet this test and enable prosecutors to successfully meet the challenge, that our present legal system is sufficiently flexible to accommodate any new technology. A small but growing number of legal scholars take the opposite view. This group argues that our present legal structure has shown itself insufficient to meet the present challenges and that the real test is yet to come.[30] Regardless of which position one takes, the simple truth is that computer-generated evidence has and will continue to run into difficulties, given our present rules of evidence and conservative approach to legal change.

A computerized record consists of patterned punch cards and magnetic or paper tapes. To be readable, it must be translated into printouts. The latter are open to attack under the common law's hearsay rule.[31] To be admissible in a trial, it must be brought in under one of the many exceptions to the hearsay rule. Since the bulk of computer-generated evidence is business records, exceptions to the rule must be in this area.

Under the old common law, business records were admissible under the shop-book rule exception. This old rule generally permitted the admission of shop records in a trial to prove amounts due. The record, however, had to be properly authenticated, and the maker of the record had to be examined by the adverse party. This old rule still survives in many local jurisdictions.

In the early 1930s, motivated by a need to make the legal structure compatible with the needs of a growing business community, the Federal Business Records Act was passed.[32] Similar legislation was later passed by about half the states. The act sets forth the following criteria for the admission of business records: (1) the records must have been made as the record of an act, transaction, occurrence, or event; (2) it must have been made in the regular course of business; and (3) it was standard procedure for this business to make a record of such an act, occurrence, transaction, or event. The legislation adopted by many states establishes substantially the same requirements.[33]

The new Federal Rules of Evidence have attempted to address themselves, at least in part, to the needs of computer-related litigation. The new rules, however, continue to retain the hearsay exclusionary rule. Critics charge that the new rules, admittedly a constructive beginning, may be too conservative to meet the future needs of highly sophisticated, computer-related litigation.

At present, the cases involving computer-generated evidence have been too few to show any discernible trend, but some courts have shown a tendency to treat computer printouts like any other form of business records. However, those cases which have been reviewed by the courts have not been clear as to the testimony necessary to provide an adequate foundation for the admission of such evidence.[34] Judges have shown a concern for the reliability of computer-stored records. Given the ease with which computers can be manipulated, there is some justification for this position. Some courts have excluded such evidence on the grounds that the individual who prepared it had no knowledge of the information fed into the computer. None of the courts that have dealt with these cases has yet handled the difficult problem of laying a proper foundation to demonstrate the reliability of a computer that arrives at complex, independently contrived conclusions.

Present computer-related litigation has involved only printouts; none of the cases has addressed the issue of whether the admission of printouts violates the confrontation or due process clauses of the Constitution. Currently, litigation remains, at best, a difficult and time-consuming matter. With the rapid growth of computer technology and its daily growing role in every facet of our lives, critics wonder whether our legal establishment will adapt the rules of evidence to this new challenge.

The computer is the workhorse of modern society. Industry relies on it; the military could not survive as a modern machine without it; and banking has come to see it as a solution to the paper glut it presently faces. Its future role shoud not be underestimated. Few inventions in this or any other century will change society as much. Law enforcement and our legal structure, however, have been slow to change and meet this new challenge. The computer has enabled criminals to steal vast fortunes, while law enforcment has slept through it all. The criminologist, too, must bear part of the blame. For many years, criminologists have shied away from studying technological crimes and those who commit them. In the coming years, either we learn to deal with computer crime or else this new class of criminals will continue to steal with impunity.

Notes

1. "Computer Crime," *National DistrictAttorneys Association Economic Crime Project Newsletter* (May-June-July 1974):189-190.

2. "Lehigh University Uncovers Payments to Alter Grades of Students," *New York Times*, September 1, 1977, p. A-18. For an excellent review of computer crime, see August Bequai, "Litigation in the Cashless Society," *Case & Comment* (November-December 1976):37; also, for a review of problems involved in computer security, see Robert S. Becker, *The Data Processing Security Game* (New York: Pergamon Press, 1977).

3. "Two Women Get Three Years in Prison for Funds Theft," *Washington Post*, June 23, 1977, p. C-4; for a review of the entire problem of computer crime, see August Bequai, *Computer Crime* (Lexington, Mass.: Lexington Books, D.C. Heath, 1977).

4. Tim A. Schabeck, "Investigators Tackle Computer Crime," *Security World* (February 1977):31; for an indepth review of the problem, see Stephen W Leibholtz and Louis D. Wilson, *Users' Guide to Computer Crime* (Radnor, Pa.: Chilton, 1974).

5. Chamber of Commerce of the United States, *White Collar Crime* (Washington, D.C.: Chamber of Commerce of the United States, 1974), p. 20.

6. Ibid., p. 7; for a further review of the problem, see U.S. Department of Justice, Law Enforcement Assistance Administration, *The Investigation of White-Collar Crime* (Washington, D.C.: Government Printing Office, 1977), pp. 199, 205.

7. "SEC Accuses Fisco of Mistating Losses to Cover-up Problems," *Wall Street Journal*, August 19, 1977, p. 20.

8. Clyde H. Fornsworth, "Fraud by Computer is Charged to Fisco," *New York Times*, August 19, 1977, p. D-1.

9. Ibid., p. D-2.

10. W. Thomas Porter, Jr., "Computer Raped by Telephone," *New York Times Magazine*, September 8, 1974, p. 35; see also, August Bequai, "The Impact of EFTS on Our Criminal Justice System," *Federal Bar Journal* (Summer-Fall 1976):190.

11. Rollin M. Perkins, *Criminal Law* (Mineola, N.Y.: Foundation Press, 1969), p. 192.

12. For a discussion of various computer crime cases, see August Bequai, *Computer Crime.*

13. "Large Loan Swindle," *Wall Street Journal*, March 12, 1976, p. 1.

14. W. Thomas Porter, Jr., "Computer Raped by Telephone," p. 35.

15. August Bequai, "The Impact of EFTS on Our Criminal Justice System," pp. 195, 196.

16. W. Thomas Porter, Jr., "Computer Raped by Telephone," p. 35; see also, Lindsay L. Baird, Jr., "Identifying Computer Vulnerability," *Data Management* (June 1974):20, 22.

17. "Computers: A New Wave," *Newsweek*, February 23, 1970, pp. 73, 74; see also, Lindsay L. Baird, Jr., "Auditing the Computer Center," *Risk Management* (August 1976):50; and Edward H. Coughran, "Evidence in Computer Cases," *The Prosecutor* XII (1977):241.

18. Tim A. Schabeck, "Investigators Tackle Computer Crime," p. 31.

19. Jerome J. Roberts, "A Practitioner's Primer on Computer-Generated Evidence," *Univ. of Chicago Law Rev.* 41 (1974): 258.

20. As the number of individuals with access to a computer system continues to grow—presently more than 2 million individuals work on computer systems—the likelihood of error and fraud will increase.

21. August Bequai, "The Impact of EFTS on Our Criminal Justice System," p. 196.

22. Jerome J. Roberts, "A Practitioner's Primer on Computer-Generated Evidence," p. 259.

23. Gerald McKnight, *Computer Crime* (New York: Walker, 1973), p. 163.

24. W. Thomas Porter, Jr., "Computer Raped by Telephone," p. 33.

25. Peter Hamilton, *Computer Security* (Philadelphia, Pa.: Auerbach, 1973), p. 29.

26. Gerald McKnight, *Computer Crime*, pp. 163, 164; see also, Gleeson I. Payne, "Equity Funding Life Insurance Company," *Forum* X (Spring 1975):1120.

27. Gerald McKnight, *Computer Crime*, pp. 144-146.

28. Chamber of Commerce of the United States, *White Collar Crime*, pp. 69-71.

29. During a series of interviews with law enforcement sources, it was made clear that computer crime is an area in which they lack expertise, especially at the local level.

30. For an indepth review of computer litigation and its surrounding problems, see August Bequai, *Computer Crime*.

31. Nancy French, "New Jersey Court Disallows NCIC Data as Evidence," *Law & Computer Technology* 8 (1975):8.

32. Jerome J. Roberts, "A Practitioner's Primer on Computer-Generated Evidence," p. 272.

33. Ibid., p. 273.

34. August Bequai, "Litigation in the Cashless Society," p. 38.

13 Environmental Offenses

In a small Eastern town, poisonous chlorine gas escaped from a local chemical plant and forced thousands of the town's citizens to flee their homes.[1] The cloud covered an area of 4500 acres and hospitalized more than half a dozen individuals for lung irritations. In a Western state, a tractor-trailer truck carrying over 40 drums full of uranium oxide overturned, spilling large amounts of this poisonous chemical.[2] More recently, the federal government disclosed that individuals who ate food that had been treated with the pesticide dibromochloropropane (DBCP) ran a risk of developing cancer.[3]

These incidents illustrate a growing area of concern for both the public and government—the environment. Protection of our soil, water, and air is no longer the concern solely of the individual citizen; it has now (especially in the post-World War II era) become the concern of law enforcement. In New York, developers have been charged under that state's laws with destroying wetlands for the construction of a housing development; a large chemical firm was found guilty of discharging chemical wastes in a river; and a small city has been criminally charged with dumping wastes in local waters.[4] Crimes against the environment constitute a new and expanding area of white-collar crime. The cost to the public is in the billions of dollars annually.[5]

Historical Development of Environmental Law

In the early common law, individuals did not own land and water rights. These belonged to the sovereign.[6] The land was held in fief or fee, and a series of rules and laws governed the relationship of the monarch with those who held land under him. This system, also known as feudalism, prevailed not only in England but also in continental Europe. Injury to either land or water was an offense against the crown. In return for the right to use the land, the occupants owed numerous obligations to their sovereign, among them military service in times of war.

By the sixteenth century, the system of feudalism had crumbled in most parts of Europe, England included. Individuals had the right to buy land and often did. In the absence of severance, a property owner's rights included not only surface rights but also rights to the area above his land and to the area below the surface.[7] However, the rights of a landowner were not without limitations. Whereas before he owed specific duties to the crown, now he had a duty to his neighbors. He was not to use his property in a manner that would cause harm to those near him.

The law of waste evolved, and in large part our environmental laws are based on these common-law developments.[8] *Waste* came to be defined as activity by the owner of the land that results in permanent damage to the land of another.[9] Three general categories of waste were established: (1) voluntary waste, (2) permissive waste, and (3) equitable waste. The first category includes damage to the land that results from an affirmative act. The second category is the result of the possessor's failure to act, when in fact he should have acted. The third category is aimed at balancing the rights of the landowner with those of his neighbors. If the owner causes damage to the property of his neighbors, and they can show that his activity was prompted by malice or reckless disregard for the rights of others, they can seek equitable relief against him. In early common law, acts of waste could result in forfeiture of an estate. Later, such acts gave rights to civil litigation aimed at compensating those who suffered.

Unlike England, where land and resources were scarce, the early settlers in this country showed little concern for the law of waste. Neighbors were far and few, and land was relatively unsettled. However, the transition occurred rapidly. In 1785 the U.S. Congress enacted legislation that provided for the appointment of surveyors to make out townships. Numerous other laws followed. This activity finally culminated in one of the major environmental laws, the Rivers and Harbors Appropriations Act of 1899.[10]

This act is one of the key tools in the battle against water pollution. The dumping of poisonous chemicals in the waterways of this country can be prosecuted under it. Section 401 of the act imposes limits on the construction of bridges, causeways, dams, or dikes and requires that such construction first be approved by the federal government. Dikes, bridges, and roadways that could endanger the environmental balance can be attacked under this section.[11]

Any type of construction on a navigable waterway requires government authorization under Section 403 of the act.[12] This section also covers harbors, canals, and havens. Section 406 provides for fines of up to $2500 and/or imprisonment of up to one year for those who violate the provisions of the act. Section 407 forbids the dumping of waste in any navigable water without the permission of the federal government. Section 411 provides for penalties for any individual or corporation who violates Section 407 of up to $2500 in fines and/or up to one year in prison. Section 413 authorizes the U.S. Justice Department to enforce the act's provisions.

Present Statutes Governing Environmental Crimes

The act of 1899 was the first of the major environmental legislative attempts to curb the pollution of our land, water, and air. Other acts, both at the federal and state level, have since been enacted. Among these is the National Environmental Policy Act of 1969 (Public Law 91-190), enacted in January 1970. Section 2 of this act defines its purpose as being to promote efforts that will safeguard the environment and "stimulate the health and welfare of man."[13] Section 101 of Title I of the act authorizes the federal government to employ all means, consistent with other national considerations, to preserve the environment.[14] Section 202 of Title II of the act authorizes the creation of an office (Council on Environmental Quality) within the executive branch of government to enforce the spirit of the act. Sections 204 and 205 set out the powers of this executive body. Among these are the power to gather data and make recommendations to the President of the United States, to consult with various governmental agencies and private bodies, and to develop national guidelines in this area.

In April 1970 the Environmental Quality Improvement Act of 1970 was enacted (Public Law 91-224).[15] Section 202 of this act notes that Congress recognizes the need for a national environmental plan, and that primary responsibility for implementing this national policy rests with both state and federal agencies.[16] Section 203 provides for the establishment of an office within the executive branch of government (Office of Environmental Quality) to assist existing federal agencies in the monitoring of environmental problems, and also to collect, analyze, and interpret data.

By the late 1950s, it became apparent that additional legislation was needed to control the pollution of our air. In 1965 the federal government amended the Clean Air Act;[17] these additional amendments give the act the necessary added muscle. Section 202 of the act gives the Environmental Protection Agency (EPA) power to set emission standards and to establish rules to regulate automobile engines. Section 204 gives the EPA power to issue subpoenas and to go to court and request that a party be enjoined from violating the act. Section 205 provides for civil penalties of up to $10,000. However, the act has been hampered by the EPA's lack of prosecutorial vigor.[18]

Another key environmental statute is the Federal Pollution Control Act, which seeks to enhance the quality and value of our water resources. Section 2 creates within the U.S. Department of the Interior an office to administer this act (the Federal Water Quality Administration). Section 3 provides for the review and analysis of water-related environmental problems, and for the development of programs to deal with this problem. The

Secretary of the Department of the Interior is authorized to investigate, with other federal agencies, water pollution problems caused by the discharge of sewage, industrial wastes, or other substances that adversely affect water.

Many states have their own environmental acts. For example, a Michigan law allows courts to adopt environmental standards for the protection of the environment where existing standards are defective.[19] The statute also allows individuals to intervene by bringing their own suits. A California law allows state agencies to refuse to issue a permit to a developer whose project will have an adverse effect on the environment.[20] Massachusetts has adopted statutes that allow state agencies to adopt regulations affecting the state's wetlands.[21] Many states have not hesitated to enforce their environmental laws. For example, Virginia has fined a housing developer for attempting to build 57 townhouses on arsenic-contaminated land.[22] The state of Maryland has brought action against one of the nation's largest steelmakers for polluting a tributary of the Chesapeake Bay.[23] The steelmaker has agreed to pay more than $500,000 in fines.

Lax Enforcement

Environmental laws are an outgrowth of our diminishing natural resources: water, air, and land. We are no longer an open frontier with unlimited energy and resources. The statutes discussed are only a beginning, and one can expect to see more. For example, the proposed amendments to the federal criminal code address the problem of pollution. Section 1853 of the proposed code (S.1437) provides for fines and criminal penalties for failure to abide by the various federal environmental acts. There have also been suggestions that publicly held corporations disclose to their stockholders corporate violations of environmental laws.[24] However, these proposals have yet to be adopted.

At the state and local level, enforcement of environmental legislation remains lax. In great part, this is due to the scarcity of the funds and manpower local prosecutors need to act.[25] At the federal level, surprisingly, environmental laws also suffer from lax enforcement. However, unlike local agencies, federal regulators have adequate funds and manpower. The problem lies with bureaucratic red tape and a lack of commitment on the part of many high officials in the federal apparatus. For example, the EPA took no action against a large firm that dumped more than 70 tons of carbon tetrachloride into the drinking water of almost 2 million people in the state of Ohio.[26]

For the last century, we have abused and polluted our environment as no other society before us. The water, land, and air that we daily use has been poisoned and contaminated and, perhaps in some cases, lost for centuries. The cost has been enormous, not only financially but also in terms of ill health and even death. Criminologists have long neglected to study or include within their scope of interest offenses against the environment. For too long, we have studied only the interaction between individuals and have neglected that between the individual and his environment. In the last analysis, it is this wider scope of activity that may determine if our civilization survives or falls. Crimes against the environment merit concern and study.

Notes

1. "Chlorine Gas Leak Forces Evacuation in Michigan Community," *Washington Post*, October 8, 1977, p. A-7.

2. Margot Hornblower, "Crash Spills Toxic Matter," *Washington Post*, October 8, 1977, p. A-1.

3. Public Citizen Staff Report, *White Collar Crime* (Washington, D.C.: Congress Watch, 1974), p. 18.

4. For a review of the cost of environmental crime, see Arnold W. Reitze, Jr., *Environmental Law* (Washington, D.C.: North American International, 1972), pp. 1-49; see also, Report of the Air Conservation Commission of the American Association for the Advancement of Science, *Air Conservation* (Washington, D.C.: American Association for the Advancement of Science, 1965) pp. 60-134.

5. William L. Burby, *Real Property* (St. Paul, Minn.: West, 1965), pp. 1-2; for an excellent review of feudal land tenure, see H.W.C. Davis, *England under the Normans and Angevins* (New York: Barnes & Noble, 1961), pp. 2-30.

6. William L. Burby, *Real Property*, pp. 13-31.

7. John E. Cribbet, William F. Fritz, and Corwin W. Johnson, *Cases and Materials on Property* (New York: Foundation Press, 1966), pp. 138-143.

8. Ibid., pp. 459-461.

9. 33 U.S.C., secs. 401, 403, 406-409, 411-415 (1970).

10. *Citizens Committee for the Hudson Valley* v. *Volpe*, 302 F.Supp. 1083 (1969).

11. *Zabel* v. *Tabb*, 430 F.2d 199 (1970).

12. 42 U.S.C., secs. 4321-4347; for a review, see Note, "Retroactive Application of the National Environmental Policy Act of 1969," *Mich. L. Rev.* 69 (1971) 732.

13. See *Environmental Defense Fund, Inc.* v. *Ruckelshaus*, 439 F.2d584 (1971); and *Moss* v. *Civil Aeronautics Board*, 430 F.2d 891 (1970).

14. 42 U.S.C.A., secs. 4372-4374.

15. For a background to the cases that gave rise to this statute, see *New Hampshire* v. *Atomic Energy Commission*, 406 F.2d 170 (1969); and *Zabel* v. *Tabb*, 430 F.2d 199 (1970).

16. 42 U.S.C.A., secs. 1857c-3 to 1857h-7.

17. For a review of the powers under the Clean Air Act, see Robert W. Martin, Jr., "Black-Listing of the Polluters," *Federal Bar Journal* 36 (Spring-Winter 1977): 17.

18. Jack Anderson and Les Whitten, "EPA Frequently Is a Paper Tiger," *Washington Post*, April 29, 1977, p. B-15; for a review of the powers under the Clean Air Act, see 33 U.S.C., secs. 1251-1376.

19. Mich. Camp. Law Ann., sec. 691.1202(2) (1972).

20. Calif. Pub. Code, 27000-27650.

21. Mass. Gen. Law, chap. 131, sec. 40; chap. 130, sec. 120.

22. Eduardo Cue, "Developer Fined for Violations at Contaminated Site," *Washington Post*, October 8, 1977, p. C-3.

23. Michael Weisskopf, "Steel Firm Fined $500,000," *Washington Post*, September 23, 1977, p.A-1.

24. Joseph M. Manko, "Environmental Disclosure—SEC vs. NEPA," *The Business Lawyer* 31 (July 1976):1907.

25. National Association of Attorneys General, *Selected Statistics on the Office of Attorney General* (Raleigh, N.C.: National Association of Attorneys General, 1975), pp. 1-18.

26. Jack Anderson and Les Whitten, "EPA Frequently Is a Paper Tiger," p. B-15.

14 Tax Frauds

In 1954 the Internal Revenue Service (IRS) began the largest investigation of tax havens in its history. The investigation, known as Operation Tradewinds, had as its target Americans who sought to evade tax payments by using trust accounts in Caribbean investment schemes.[1] An offshoot of this investigation was Project Haven, which focused on the activities of the Castle Bank and Trust Company, with branches in Nassau and the Cayman Islands.[2] The investigation involved hundreds of Americans, many of them prominent figures in the world of sports and show business. Since its inception, the investigation provided information the IRS used to levy tax penalties against more than one hundred individuals.[3]

In a separate case, a prominent New York architect pleaded guilty in federal court to charges of income tax evasion.[4] The defendant was also the president of a small company. He laundered more than $30,000 of his company's income through a scheme involving a well-known Washington, D.C. attorney and a well-known figure in the world of pornography. The latter was paid fees for alleged services involving interior decoration. The Washington, D.C. lawyer was paid fees for allegedly providing services in the area of public relations. The two individuals would then return the money to the defendant, minus a percentage for their services as fronts for tax purposes.

These cases serve to illustrate a growing and often neglected area of white-collar crime—tax frauds. Tax evasion costs the government more than $30 billion annually.[5] One former IRS Commissioner has noted that we "face a real danger of general deterioration" of our revenue system if the trend continues.[6] In part, the enforcement of the tax laws has been lax and is directly responsible for this growing problem.[7] In one particular year, more than 1000 IRS investigations were shelved because of bureaucratic difficulty, shortages of resources, or political interference.[8] The problem is serious, increasing rapidly, and one that merits close scrutiny for public policy reasons. If nations cannot raise revenue to meet their needs, the institutions and programs that have been geared for their citizenry must either falter or be supported by a smaller tax base. In essence, the honest minority would be taxed heavily in order to support themselves, as well as the non-paying majority.

History of Our Tax Laws

In 1913 the Sixteenth Amendment became effective. It empowered the U.S. Congress to "lay and collect taxes on incomes, whatever source derived."[9] Shortly thereafter, the IRS was assigned the task of securing compliance and bringing to prosecution willful evaders of the federal income tax statutes.[10] In fiscal 1913 the federal income tax constituted a minor percent of all federal receipts. However, after World War II, the federal income tax produced more than 50 percent of all federal revenue.

Taxation first became an issue in the early years of the Republic. In 1794 the U.S. Congress passed a tax on carriages. The challenge to this law came in the case of *Hylton* v. *United States* in 1796, but the U.S. Supreme Court ruled that the tax was constitutional.[11] Until the Civil War, however, the income tax played no role in the federal budget. Custom receipts and the sale of public lands formed the basis of the federal tax structure.[12] During the Civil War, both the Confederacy and the Union were forced to seek other sources for funding their war machines; both governments levied an income tax.

After the war, the income tax was repealed as a result of great pressure from the business community. Eastern business interests saw it as a form of "communism."[13] However, agrarian and labor groups pressed for a restoration of the income tax. The Populists, led by William Jennings Bryan, finally pressured the Congress into passing a new income tax law. The law of 1894 soon faced its first challenge in the case of *Pollock* v. *Farmers' Loan & Trust Company.*[14] The case involved a suit by a stockholder asking a New York Federal court to enjoin his company from paying taxes under the new law. The court refused, and the case soon found its way to the U.S. Supreme Court, which held that the 1894 law was unconstitutional.

The Spanish-American War raised pressure, once again, by labor and agrarian groups for a new income tax law. The large profits of the business giants further reinforced the pressure on the Congress. In 1913 the Congress passed the Revenue Act, which imposed a tax on the income of individuals and corporations. With the new law came attempts by both individuals and corporate entities to evade it. More than 60 years later, the IRS would begin an investigation into the largest automobile maker in this country.[15] The company, with sales exceeding $40 billion annually, posed a serious challenge to the IRS' capability to police and enforce the tax laws of the nation. Charges and countercharges have been made by both sides. The case revolves around the value of the company's "expense material."[16] The company's estimate was at $191 million; that of the IRS was put at $465 million. The outcome may well determine the ability of the IRS to audit large firms.

Criminal Laws

The IRS is a part of the U.S. Treasury Department and has more than 50 district offices throughout the country. However, the enforcement of its laws is handled by the Intelligence Division (ID), which consists of more than 2000 special agents. Only the ID has the authority and jurisdiction to conduct criminal investigations involving the federal tax laws. This division is armed with an arsenal of statutes that can be employed in a variety of ways to combat the problem of tax frauds.

The Internal Revenue Code makes it a misdemeanor to "willfully" fail to file a timely tax return.[17] To establish its case, the IRS must prove, beyond a reasonable doubt,[18] that the defendant was: (1) required to file a return, (2) that none was filed, and (3) that the failure to do so was "willful."

An attempt to "evade or defeat" any tax or its payment is a felony under the Internal Revenue Code.[19] However, the IRS must show that the defendant: (1) took steps to evade the tax, and (2) that these acts were willful. The IRS must also show that as a result of the defendant's activity, the government lost some tax revenue. The Code has been used successfully to prosecute various forms of white-collar crime. Few white-collar criminals pay tax on all their illicit income. If properly implemented, the Code could be a powerful tool in the government's arsenal.

The filing of a fraudulent tax return with the IRS is a felony under the Internal Revenue Code.[20] The federal prosecutors must prove two elements to obtain a conviction: (1) the defendant filed a fraudulent tax return, and (2) he did so willfully. The fraudulent filing, however, must be of a "material" nature. The IRS agents need not show that the defendant took any "affirmative steps" in this instance (as is the case in tax evasion cases), but only that a false return was filed.

Investigatory Sources

IRS agents rely, as do other investigators, on a variety of sources to detect tax frauds. A key source is the informer. Project Haven was made possible by the assistance of informers.[21] Other government agencies—local and federal—can refer cases to the IRS field offices. Newspapers are also important sources to detecting tax frauds. In addition, the Audit Division of the IRS may refer cases to the ID.

Some of the methods used to perpetrate tax frauds involve using double sets of books. A corporation or an individual may keep one set of books that details the actual earnings and income and another set of records for purposes of misleading the IRS and paying lower taxes. For example, a New

England businessman evaded higher taxes by simply not reporting more than $1 million in income. In another case, a physician evaded more than $60,000 in taxes by maintaining a double set of books. In New York City, a physician was indicted for evading more than $30,000 in taxes.

Felons also constantly shift their funds from one bank to another. Sometimes, foreign accounts are opened, and funds are shifted to them in an attempt to confuse IRS agents. In addition, foreign banks need not honor IRS subpoenas, thus making it extremely difficult to obtain incriminating evidence against the target of an investigation.

Tax evaders also employ fake invoices, deduct fictitious expenses, and may conceal assets by placing them in the names of friends, relatives, or even shell corporations. Records and books are also occasionally destroyed, making prosecution even more difficult.

IRS Audit

Inquiries by the IRS take on two forms: (1) office inquiries, and (2) field investigations. An office inquiry involves a letter or telephone contact from the local IRS office. The taxpayer may be asked several questions or requested to supply supporting documents. The inquiry is usually informal and done through the mail. The field investigation, however, is formal. IRS agents may visit the taxpayer at his home or office and ask to review his books and records. A field investigation may be an indication that the taxpayer is the target of a criminal investigation.

Several years ago, an office inquiry that eventually led to a field investigation resulted in the prosecution of the chief executive officer of a major hospital in the Southern United States. In 1970 the hospital received a $62 million loan from the Federal Housing Administration for expansion of its physical facilities. An IRS formal investigation later disclosed that the defendant and several associates had defrauded the government of more than $800,000 in taxes.

Audits, however, raise certain key legal issues. For example, what are the rights of a suspect in an IRS investigation? How does an audit touch upon the suspect's relations with various professionals he comes to rely on and consult with? IRS investigations, because they are both civil and criminal in nature, raise crucial issues.

One of the key questions in IRS investigations concerns the rights of the suspect when consulting with professionals: the attorney-client privilege. However, that privilege is qualified in tax fraud investigations. For example, if the client has consulted with his attorney in connection with a legal problem, that communication is privileged.[22] However, if the attorney and the client discuss a joint business venture, although the individual may also be a client, the communication is not privileged.[23] If the communication is relayed to a third party, the privilege is waived.[24] The privilege also does not apply in situations in which the attorney merely prepared a tax return.[25]

There is no accountant-client privilege.[26] The workpapers of an accountant relating to the client are not privileged and may be subpoenaed by the IRS. If, however, the accountant acts as an agent of the attorney and prepares papers in a matter involving the attorney's client, the papers could be privileged.[27] The suspect cannot raise his Fifth Amendment right against compulsory self-incrimination to the IRS in an attempt to prevent his accountant from surrendering such workpapers. However, save for certain features that are unique to IRS investigations, the individual has an array of constitutional rights at his disposal in tax fraud audits.

Proving Tax Frauds

The burden of proving a tax fraud rests with the government. However, the IRS need not show probable cause for suspecting fraud in order to audit a taxpayer's records, even those which might otherwise be barred by the statute of limitations.[28] The statute does not begin to run until the taxpayer has filed a return for the taxable year.[29] Once the statute is tolled, the government has three years within which to bring its case to court.

Proof of tax fraud must be beyond a reasonable doubt. When the government has obtained a confession or has a number of witnesses who can testify to the fraud, the matter can be handled appropriately. Unfortunately, this is not always the case. In complex frauds, there are few witnesses and those who have knowledge of the events may not be willing to communicate with the government. Further, confessions are more difficult to obtain since the suspect is usually educated and sufficiently sophisticated to know what his legal rights are.

In some tax fraud cases, the defendant has either failed to disclose all his income or has claimed fictitious deductions. These are usually the types of tax frauds the IRS is capable of prosecuting. In such cases, IRS agents attempt to isolate and identify these omissions or fictitious deductions and verify the statements. Access to a defendant's books and records usually facilitate the process. The IRS need only show that the defendant did not disclose these additional sources of income. It is possible that these funds are located in a secret account or recorded on a second set of books. Witnesses may also come forth and inform on the defendant. In cases of false deductions, the IRS usually attempts to determine the truth and, in the process, is able to specifically outline the fraud. Proving willful intent is no difficult matter in such cases.

However, in cases where the defendant has either destroyed his records or keeps them beyond the reach of the IRS, fraud is somewhat more difficult to prove. The government must reconstruct the true financial position of the individual or the events as they transpired. Agents must interview witnesses and obtain records. Financial statements provided by the defendant to financial institutions may also be of value in reconstructing the defendant's financial position. Real estate records, bank records, past tax returns, etc. all assist the agent in reconstructing a defendant's financial history and worth. This is no easy task, since a sophisticated white-collar felon knows his rights and has the assistance of a battery of professional talent. The investigator, keeping all this in mind, proceeds with caution. As a result of a recent IRS investigation, a corporate suspect has accused the government's agents of having harrassed, abused, and intimidated its employees.[30] The accusations have served to place the IRS on the defensive and have caused extensive delays in the investigation.

Tax frauds are a serious and growing problem. Successful tax evasions have the effect of forcing the government to cut back on services and to tax the honest at a higher rate. A modern state cannot survive as a viable political entity without a tax base. However, the IRS faces very serious problems. A recent study shows that its investigations and prosecutions have concentrated on "petty cheaters" rather than the major tax evaders.[31] By failing to go after the "big cheaters," the IRS may have missed a potential $1.5 billion in additional revenue in one year alone.[32] Further, the study found that although the IRS increased its audit of smaller businesses from 1.1 to 2.5 percent, its audit of the larger firms decreased by 15 percent.[33] The audits of multinational corporations have decreased by as much as 40 percent.[34] One former IRS agent has charged that the IRS lacks the capability to audit the giant multinational firms.[35] As an example, he noted that the IRS had failed to collect more than $2 billion from the American Telephone & Telegraph Company because of its inability to do a complete audit of the corporation.

Many critics also charge that federal prosecutors have shown a lack of prosecutorial vigor, especially in cases involving large corporations. Judges, too, have shown little vigor in meting out punishment in tax fraud cases. For example, the likelihood of imprisonment in tax frauds is only 36.5 percent when compared to 91.8 percent in bank robbery cases.[36] A physician who had concealed more than $80,000 in income over a three-year period was only ordered to pay a fine.[37] A businessman who had concealed $100,000 in income over a three-year period was only fined $2500.[38] These penalties are hardly a deterrence to other felons.

Tax frauds can have significant social and economic ramifications; many societies are currently facing this dilemma. However, few societies possess the technological capability and sophistication found in the United States. That capability has enabled corporations to grow into ministates. It has also enabled educated and sophisticated felons to devise tax frauds for which the IRS is ill-prepared to investigate or prosecute. Computer technology, for example, enables felons to maintain several sets of records. The IRS needs to modify its tactics and strategy in order to meet the challenge. At present, save for a few "petty cheaters," the rest get away.

Notes

1. Jack Anderson and Les Whitten, "Alexander Hampered Tax Probe," *Washington Post*, October 25, 1976, p. C-15.
2. Ibid.; see also, Larry Kramer, "The IRS and Its Briefcase Caper," *New York Times*, January 30, 1977, p. F-2.
3. Ibid.
4. "Architect Pleads Guilty to Tax Evasion Charges Involving Brothel Owner," *New York Times*, September 22, 1977, p. B-2.
5. Public Citizen Staff Report, *White Collar Crime* (Washington, D.C.: Congress Watch, 1974), pp. 17, 18.
6. Ibid.
7. Ibid.
8. Ibid.
9. U.S. Const., Amend. XVI.
10. Comments, "Immunity of the Individual's Tax Records from Search and Seizure—Judicial Offspring of a Fourth and Fifth Amendment Intimacy," *Univ. of San Francisco L. Rev.* 8 (1973):55.
11. 3 U.S. (3 Dall.) 171 (1796).
12. Boris I. Bittker and Lawrence M. Stone, *Federal Income Estate and Gift Taxation* (Boston: Little Brown, 1972), p. 4.
13. Ibid., p. 5.
14. 157 U.S. 429 (1895).
15. "Treated Like Gangsters, GM Says of Fraud Probe," *Washington Post*, June 22, 1977, pp. D-9, D-10.
16. Ibid., p. D-10.
17. Int. Rev. Code, Sec. 7203.
18. *Helvering* v. *Mitchell*, 303 U.S. 391 (1938).
19. Int. Rev. Code, sec. 7201.
20. Ibid., sec. 7206.
21. Larry Kramer, "The IRS and Its Briefcase Caper," p. F-2.
22. *United States* v. *Finley*, 434 F.2d 596 (5th Cir. 1970).
23. Ibid.
24. *United States* v. *McDonald*, 313 F.2d 832 (2d Cir. 1963).
25. *United States* v. *Merrell*, 303 F.Supp. 490 (N.D.N.Y. 1969).
26. *Couch* v. *United States*, 409 U.S. 322 (1973).

27. *United States* v. *Judson*, 322 F.2d 460 (9th Cir. 1963).

28. *United States* v. *Powell*, 379 U.S. 48 (1964).

29. *Ryan* v. *United States*, 379 U.S. 61 (1964).

30. "Treated Like Gangsters, GM Says of Fraud Probe," pp. D-9, D-10.

31. Nancy L. Ross, "Nader Says IRS Is Soft on Fat Cats," *Washington Post*, November 15, 1976, p. D-11.

32. Ibid.

33. Ibid.

34. Ibid.

35. Ibid.

36. John A. Jenkins and Robert H. Rhode, *White-Collar Justice—A BNA Special Report* (Washington, D.C.: Bureau of National Affairs, 1976), p. 11.

37. Ibid.

38. Ibid., p. 10

15 Influx of Organized Crime

In the District of Columbia, the police infiltrated and identified a large gambling ring only to find that many of its members were well-known professionals, including several Congressional officials.[1] At one of Washington, D.C.'s plush apartment buildings, gambling operations running into the thousands of dollars were so common that a well-known U.S. Senator finally complained to the authorities.[2] In California, investigators were looking into charges that Mexican-American gangsters were strong-arming local community-based programs into paying them large sums of money as consulting fees.[3] In Pennsylvania, federal prosecutors charged five individuals, two of them related to a reputed Mafia chieftain, with being involved in a $13 million insurance fraud.[4]

Organized crime is a serious problem of epic proportions and has permeated, as the preceding examples serve to illustrate, every facet and strata of our society. It controls businesses that bring in billions of dollars annually;[5] federal authorities place the figure as high as $50 billion.[6] In one city alone, organized crime-related figures had investments in numerous businesses, with total assets of over a half billion dollars and revenue of over $800 million annually.[7] The income of organized crime exceeds that of any legitimate single sector of our economy.[8] It is a growing business, and one that threatens our very democratic fiber. Today's crime chieftain is a sophisticated investor who looks upon crime as a business. More and more, the organized criminal elements have made their way into the area of white-collar crime. Presently, much of their activities can be characterized as involving white-collar crimes.[9]

Development and Rise of Organized Crime

The very mention of the words *organized crime* evokes in the average citizen pictures of a secret conspiracy by a handful of individuals who meet in dark rooms and plot the destruction of society. Some law enforcement authorities speak of organized crime in terms of a national conspiracy, dominated by a small group of ethnic elements.[10] Although many definitions have been offered to explain this phenomenon that we call *organized crime*, in general, I would define it as being illegal behavior on the part of organized groups from all strata of our society working either alone or with

129

one or more other organized groups with the objective of gaining economic and political power.

Organized criminal activity is not new, nor is it entirely an American phenomenon. Secret societies such as the Assassins (in Persia) and the numerous terrorist groups of the Mediterranean world have long been with us. One of the first organized criminal groups in this country was headed by Pierre Moreau (the "Moll"), a French-Canadian who ran the first illegal distillery in eighteenth century America. The nineteenth century saw the rise and proliferation of organized criminal activity not only in the cities, but also in rural America. While the cities gave rise to such groups as the O'Connell Guards and Bowery Boys in New York and the Hounds and Sydney Ducks in San Francisco, armed groups rose also in such rural places as Johnson County, Wyoming. In 1890 an Irish widow brought an action against a Chicago-based association for malicious interference with her business; apparently, she was not too insignificant to attract the attention of the larger, criminally oriented association. By the turn of the century, these isolated and small business organizations began to grow and to become a strong, though unrecognized, business force in the American economic and political systems.

The turn of the century saw large groups of immigrants coming to this country. The cities changed hands, and political bosses, with large ethnic constituencies, began to assume the levers of power. The gangs served the political czars, thus ensuring that the vote was out in force. However, during this period, organized crime itself began to employ the new technology that had been developed during the latter part of the nineteenth century. The new media of telephonic communications, mass transportation, and the growing electronic revolution enabled these localized criminal syndicates to work together nationally. The gambling operations that would later take on national dimensions, as well as various business-related frauds, were to be made possible by this new technology.

Until 1934, organized crime in this country was fragmented and in turmoil. The Mafia groups, as well as the Neapolitan Camorra and the numerous Jewish and Irish gangs, were still at odds. The early 1930s saw war between the various American-Sicilian gangster groups; the conflict came to be called the Castellamare War. At the end of the conflict, the old "mustache Petes" who had dominated the Mafia groups in this country gave way to new and aggressive leadership.[11] Soon after, national instruments were established to resolve conflicts between these various criminal groups; even internal policing mechanisms were set up to ensure discipline. A national syndicate made its appearance, armed with the machinery of modern technology. With the techniques of modern business, this new group made its way into the world of politics and industry.

Areas of Organized Criminal Activities

There are two key areas of organized criminal involvement: (1) areas of traditional concern to organized crime, and (2) areas of growing concern and penetration. The former are usually associated with such ventures as drugs, gambling, loan sharking, and theft of cargo; the latter activities are usually connected to the world of business and politics. Funds from traditional criminal sources have been used with increasing success to fund fraudulent operations in the business and political arenas. The movement of these funds has been so successful that one of the nation's largest hotel chains is controlled by organized crime.

The drug aspect of organized crime requires a historical perspective in order to fully understand the present state of affairs. Morphine, one of the first anesthetics of modern medicine, was first discovered in 1805; during the period of the American Civil War, the hypodermic needle was invented and morphine was widely used to ease the pain of wounded soldiers. A class of morphine addicts soon arose; they were said to be suffering the "soldier's illness," since many of them were veterans of the war. In 1898 German chemists were able to synthesize a "miracle" drug that could alleviate the pain and suffering of those addicted to morphine; the new drug was heroin.

As the problem of addiction grew both in this country and abroad, religious and reformist groups joined hands to enact legislation to curtail its use. In 1914 the U.S. Congress enacted the Harrison Act; its objective was to control the broad dissemination of narcotics. Within the next several years, the courts interpreted the act as disallowing the dispensing of these drugs to addicts.[12] Inevitably, a black market emerged that could meet the needs of this large addict population. The market presently realizes over $5 billion annually and constitutes more than 500,000 active users. This trade in drugs, well organized and financed by criminal syndicates, has, in turn, been effectively employed to build a vast business and political empire.[13] Prohibition in the 1920s gave organized crime its first big "boost"; the narcotic trade has ensured its place in our society as a power to contend with.

Gambling, another activity of organized crime, is a multibillion dollar annual business; it is a key source of funds for organized crime. It encompasses lotteries, off-track race horse betting, illegal gambling establishments, and betting on various assorted sporting events. In some neighborhoods, gambling operations account for large numbers of jobs. It corrupts law enforcement and ensures organized crime some public acceptance.

Loan sharking is another traditional area of organized criminal activity. Funds are loaned at high rates to various individuals; the latter may be legitimate businessmen who have no other sources of financing or gamblers who have fallen on hard times. Through this vehicle, organized crime has also made its way into the business world. For example, a major Mafia figure was indicted in a large Eastern city with several other individuals when he coerced the owner of a multimillion dollar poultry business to relinquish control of the firm to him.[14] One of the owners of the company had fallen into debt and had put up the firm as collateral. In a more illustrative case, a meat packing firm fell under the control of organized crime and was bilked, together with its creditors, of more than $1 million.[15] Bankruptcy frauds are many times tied to loan sharking operations. When the borrower fails to keep up with his payments, the criminals take control of the collateral—in most cases, his business.

Thefts involving cargo at both airports and seaports are common and exceed $1 billion annually.[16] Organized crime has an efficient network of fences who sell the stolen cargo to both businesses and individual members of the public. As an example, one afternoon at 4:30 P.M. some cargo was stolen while en route to a designated location.[17] The cargo was illegally, but profitably, disposed of by 5:15 P.M. that same day. Theft of cargo may also account for as much as 20 percent of all cigarettes sold in New York City.[18] It is an important source of revenue and one that keeps an elaborate and national fencing mechanism in daily operation.

Organized crime has evolved and has made its way into both business and political arenas. These criminals have mastered the techniques of the white-collar felon. For example, in an elaborate business fraud involving federal loan programs, organized criminal elements were able to obtain loans exceeding $500,000 from the federal government.[19] The Medicare program, affecting nursing homes and estimated to be worth $10 billion, is also presently under attack and has been infiltrated by organized criminal elements.[20] They have also made their way into the area of computer technology. The director of the Illinois Bureau of Investigation has warned that with the aid of insiders, organized crime figures have been able to manipulate computers and transfer funds into accounts under their control.

Labor unions also pose a tempting target for organized crime. With pension funds amounting to more than $100 billion, unions have fallen victim to these criminal elements. Such funds have been used to assist organized crime figures in gaining control of businesses, as well as political figures. Further, the sheer number of potential votes makes labor unions a tempting prize; it also ensures that with this arsenal of potential votes, organized crime can elect its own political representatives. In addition, the threat of strikes ensures payoffs from businessmen who want labor peace. For example, federal investigators are presently looking into payments made by employers to dock worker unions as a guarantee of labor peace.[21] One union official alone is alleged to have received more than $80,000 in two years in such payoffs. The practice is said to be prevalent. The U.S. Labor Department, charged with policing this area, has proven ineffective and lax in enforcing present laws. Further, just as other federal investigatory bodies, it must refer all criminal cases to the Justice Department for prosecution, since it only has civil jurisdiction; this hardly suffices in the war against well-organized criminal elements.

Organized Crime Act

In the fall of 1975, the governor of Maryland and several of his business associates were indicted on 20 counts of mail fraud and two counts, involving Sections 1961, 1962, and 1963, of the Organized Crime Control Act.[22] The act, passed in 1970, has as its objective the curtailing of activities of organized criminals; it was enacted to circumvent some of the past problems law enforcement faced when attempting to prosecute racketeering activities.

Section 1961 defines *racketeering activity* to include a broad range of activities in which organized crime is found: bribery, extortion, counterfeiting, embezzlement from pension and welfare funds, obstruction of justice, and many others. Section 1962 makes it unlawful to receive any income derived from racketeering, to acquire control over any business or enterprise engaged in interstate or foreign commerce through racketeering activity, and to conduct any business engaged in interstate or foreign commerce through a pattern of racketeering activities.

Section 1963 provides for criminal penalties for anyone convicted under the act of up to $25,000 in fines and/or up to 20 years imprisonment. Further, the convicted felon must forfeit to the federal government any property he has acquired or maintained in violation of the act. Section 1964 provides for federal courts to issue restraining orders to prevent violation of section 1962; further, any individual who has been injured as a result of the racketeering activities of another may bring civil suit and recover treble damages against the defendant, plus the costs associated with his suit.

These statutes are a powerful tool when properly employed against organized crime figures. Federal prosecutors, however, have made little use of them. These statutes can also be employed in white-collar crime cases, thus enabling federal prosecutors to check the growth of organized crime in this arena. The act not only punishes convicted felons, but also provides for forfeiture of their illegally obtained profits.

Organized crime affects every facet of our society—all classes and groups. It is not the preserve of any one ethnic group but is a confederation of numerous criminal elements working together when necessity dictates. It is a national criminal conspiracy that attacks and undermines all levels of our economic and political spectrum. It has made inroads in the white-collar crime area and has carried with it the violence and arrogance of an earlier time. Organized crime must be attacked and prosecuted vigorously. The tools it employs are increasingly those of the white-collar felon; in turn, law enforcement should employ the statutes available to it in this area. For example, the antitrust statutes could be effective, if employed aggressively, in this forum; the antifraud provisions of the securities laws could also be employed effectively. Organized crime has changed; we too, must change our perception and strategy when confronting it.

Notes

1. Timothy S. Robinson, "Gambling Ring Operators Convicted," *Washington Post,* October 15, 1977, p. A-1.

2. Frank Browning, "Organized Crime in Washington," *Washingtonian Magazine,* April 1976, pp. 96-97.

3. John Berthelson, "California Probing Chicano Mafia," *Washington Post,* March 6, 1977, p. A-1.

4. "Insurance Fraud," *Washington Post,* June 9, 1976, p. A-3.

5. Jack Anderson, "The Shadow of the Mafia Over Our Government," *Parade Magazine,* August 7, 1977, p. 8.

6. Chamber of Commerce of the United States, *Deskbook on Organized Crime* (Washington, D.C.: Chamber of Commerce of the United States, 1972), p. 6.

7. Ibid., p. 7.

8. Ibid., p. 6.

9. Based on my interviews with investigators and prosecutors.

10. Based on my interviews with law enforcement sources; see also, Paul S. Meskil, "Meet the New Godfather," *New York Magazine,* February 28, 1977, p. 28; and The President's Commission on Law Enforcement and Administration of Justice, *Task Force Report on Organized Crime* (Washington, D.C.: Government Printing Office, 1976), pp. 5, 6.

11. For a study of the Mafia's historical development, see Anton Blok, *The Mafia of a Sicilian Village, 1860-1960* (New York: Harper & Row, 1974), pp. 5-17.

12. *Jim Fuy May* v. *United States,* 254 U.S. 189 (1920); also *United States* v. *Daremus,* 249 U.S. 86 (1919).

13. The President's Commission on Law Enforcement and Administration of Justice, *Task Force Report on Organized Crime,* pp. 3, 4.

14. "A Reputed Mafia Figure Accused with Seven of a Plot to Seize Bronx Concern," *New York Times,* August 26, 1977, p. A-13.

15. National Institute of Law Enforcement and Criminal Justice, *Anatomy of a Scam: A Case Study of a Planned Bankruptcy by Organized Crime* (Washington, D.C.: Government Printing Office, 1976), p. 21.

16. U.S. Department of Transportation, *Cargo Theft and Organized Theft* (Washington, D.C.: Government Printing Office, 1972), p. 9.

17. Ibid., pp. 38-39.

18. Ibid., p. 39.

19. Jack Anderson, "The Shadow of the Mafia Over Our Government," p. 9.

20. Based on my interviews with law enforcement sources.

21. "U.S. Subpoenas Transway International, R.J. Reynolds Unit in Dock Crime Probe," *Wall Street Journal,* November 28, 1977, p. 4.

22. See 18 U.S.C., secs. 1961-1968.

 # The Problems of Investigators

A Prince Georges County, Maryland, grand jury indicted the sheriff and his assistant in an alleged scheme to misappropriate county funds.[1] The grand jury also charged that the sheriff's office had cheated, misused jail trustees for personal gain, and had lied. In addition, the grand jury found that the sheriff's deputies were "undereducated and untrained." In a separate investigation involving one of the nation's largest urban police forces, it was reported that detectives refused to handle difficult cases.[2] It appears that the detective bureau was concerned that its failure to make arrests would hurt its performance record. Detectives sent back more than 30 percent of all cases sent to them by other divisions.[3]

There are more than 30,000 law enforcement agencies in the United States, covering a motley of county, city, state, and federal agencies. Their roles vary, but they all have one common element: prosecutors, whether local or federal, rely on them to investigate and bring cases to their attention for prosecution. Without this investigatory apparatus, the prosecutorial machinery would cease to function. The investigators, however, are ill-trained and poorly equipped for the task of combatting white-collar crimes. Many of these agencies are further handicapped by corruption and political interference in their everyday operations.[4] Such an apparatus has, and will continue to have, difficulty in meeting the challenge of white-collar felons.

Development of Law Enforcement

Moll Cutpurse (1584-1659) was legendary in her own time. She ran one of London's more sophisticated and successful seventeenth century fencing operations. Plays were written about Moll, and the local populace nicknamed her the "Queen Regent of Misrule." Law enforcement officials knew of her existence but left her alone. Moll fell into the clutches of the law only when she entered politics and sided with the losing party.

Not to be outdone by Moll, the eighteenth century gave rise to Jonathan Wilde (1683-1725), the colorful and somewhat dishonest sheriff of London. Jonathan was both the top law enforcement official for the city and also the head of the underworld. The eighteenth century had as yet not given birth to a professional police force. Law enforcement was in the hands of individuals known as "thief-takers." Many of these were part-time thiefs themselves. They were empowered to make arrests and, on occasion, received some private rewards for their deeds. A system of informers and middlemen negotiated the return of stolen property. Jonathan had many enemies; and in May 1725, as fate would have it, he was hanged for a crime he did not commit, or so he said.

Until the turn of the nineteenth century, law enforcement was largely a private matter. There were no professional police forces in the United States or England. Parliamentarians feared that a strong, professional police force might give rise to a dictatorial government, similar to what had occurred in continental Europe. The kings might employ it to imprison their enemies. Further, the basic concern of jurists was with escaped peasants, well into the seventeenth century.[5] During the eighteenth century, jurists began to concentrate some of their efforts on the problem of "rogues, vagabonds, and beggars."[6] The growth of urbanism in the early nineteenth century brought initial efforts to change the structure of law enforcement.

During the early part of the nineteenth century, most localities employed constables to police their streets. The constable only worked during daytime hours and investigated only those crimes which were brought to his attention.[7] A nightwatch, composed of volunteers, patrolled the streets at night. By the 1850s, this quasi-professional system began to change. After the Civil War, a professional police force emerged. However, criminologists concentrated their efforts, and were thus able to influence the new rising professional police forces, in the area of traditional crimes—offenses usually committed by the poor. Scholars of police science, like William D. Morrison (1852-1943), concentrated their efforts on crimes of the lower classes.[8] As a result, the developing police science was cast in their mold.

By 1900 the economic dynamism that had advanced rapidly after the Civil War met with opposition from many groups in this country. The farmers of the Midwest were tired of the abuses of the railroads, and the middle class of the cities grew tired of the price fixing in all industries. Beginning in 1898, federal laws were passed to address this problem. Bureaucracies with national police jurisdiction were assigned the task of policing various sectors of the economy; the first of these was the Interstate Commerce Commission (ICC). It was soon followed in 1905 by the Federal Trade Commission (FTC); and an array of other federal policing agencies arose during the 1930s: the Securities Exchange Commission (SEC), the Civil Aeronautics Board (CAB), the Maritime Commission (MC), and so on. At present, there are two basic police structures: (1) the local and (2) the federal.[9]

Local Police Forces

In 1931 the Wickersham Commission, concerned with the highly fragmented structure of local police forces, recommended a pooling of resources.[10] In spite of these recommendations, local law enforcement agencies have continued to multiply and diversify. One recent presidential commission has noted that:

. . . America is . . . a nation of small police forces, each operating independently within the limits of its jurisdiction. . . .[11]

The counties alone have more than 17,000 police departments, and over 60 percent of these employ less than 10 full-time employees.[12] A study of 1597 local police departments found that only 7 percent employed more than 100 employees, 38 percent employed between 10 and 99 employees, and 55 percent employed 9 or fewer employees.[13] Another study has shown that only about one-half of the more than 30,000 local jurisdictions have police departments, and of these, over 50 percent employ fewer than 10 officials.[14] At the local level, serious questions have been raised as to whether these law enforcement agencies can meet the minimum demands of traditional policing, let alone the investigatory needs raised by white-collar felons.

Traditionally, local law enforcement forces have been composed of sheriffs, highway police, state police, traffic police, game wardens, liquor officials, constables, marshalls, and commissions. All these structures have fulfilled, and continue to fulfill, the need to investigate local crimes. In general, most police forces direct their energies in the area of traditional offenses, such as keeping order, monitoring traffic, settling family quarrels, and finding lost children and even lost pets. They are viewed as service agencies more than law enforcement apparatuses. In large part, this is a role they have sought and welcomed in the past. Much of current police science still clings to this view.[15]

Police departments in large urban areas usually concentrate their efforts in seven key areas: (1) homicide, (2) sex offenses, (3) robbery, (4) aggravated assault, (5) burglary, (6) larceny, and (7) auto thefts.[16] Few urban centers have fraud units, and those which do either commit minimal resources and funds to this area or continue to concentrate their efforts in the traditional crime sector and create specialized "fraud branches" for cosmetic purposes.[17] For example, the District of Columbia recently set up a Consumer Fraud Unit within the Check Fraud Section. The unit is accredited with having brought some 97 cases for criminal prosecution.[18] However, no information is available on what type of cases these were and the amounts of dollars involved. In fact, the unit is too small, ill-trained, and poorly equipped to successfully combat white-collar crimes.[19] Fraud-related arrests in the District of Columbia usually account for fewer than 1 percent of all police arrests.[20]

The role of local law enforcement continues as it has in the past: the investigation and bringing to prosecution of traditional criminal cases. The police will investigate crimes brought to their attention by informers, members of the public, and those which they themselves have witnessed.

The decision to arrest is usually theirs, although the issuance of warrants is a prosecutorial function. Suspects are usually detained for questioning before a decision is made to place them under arrest. As a rule, investigations are simple and involve only a handful of individuals. There are exceptions, such as gambling- and drug-related crimes. However, by standards of training and education, local law enforcement agencies are ill-equipped to handle sophisticated white-collar crimes. The fragmented nature of local police forces makes their investigation of white-collar crimes extremely difficult. Unlike traditional offenses, these crimes require extensive investigative resources in terms of manpower, funds, and the requisite training. Local police forces lack these capabilities, and as a result, the task of investigating and bringing to prosecution white-collar offenses lies with the federal investigatory apparatus.[21]

Federal Cops

At the national level, the investigatory apparatus is divided into two general categories: (1) Congressional investigators, and (2) investigators of the executive branch. Congressional committees and subcommittees (from both houses) have their own investigators. These committees hold hearings on various matters that are of interest to Congress.[22] Witnesses are either invited to testify or subpoenaed. Section 3486, Title 18, of the United States Code authorizes these committees to grant immunity to witnesses testifying before them. Section 1505 provides for penalties of up to $5000 in fines and/or up to five years imprisonment for anyone who "corruptly, or by threats or force, or by any threatening letter or communication" intimidates or interferes with Congressional investigations or witnesses.

Section 3486 provides for prosecution of witnesses who perjure themselves before Congressional committees. Prosecution, however, is a prerogative of the executive wing of government and is conducted by the U.S. Justice Department. For example, former Central Intelligence Agency (CIA) Director Richard Helms was recently prosecuted and plead "no contest" to misdemeanor charges for having perjured himself before a Senate committee that was investigating CIA activities in Latin America.[23] Unfortunately, these committees are limited in their efficiency by the inner political differences of those who sit on them;[24] an additional hindrance is the fact that if the Justice Department refuses to prosecute, these Congressional investigative bodies have no recourse other than perhaps to exert political pressure on the executive branch.

At the executive end, there are more than 2000 different agencies, departments, commissions, and committees.[25] These have specific responsibility for policing and regulating various sectors of the national economy.

The executive investigatory apparatus can be divided into two major areas: (1) departments, agencies, and divisions that are not independent of the executive branch of government, and (2) agencies and boards that enjoy a semiautonomous independence from the executive branch of government.[26] The latter are also known as independent regulatory agencies.

The nonindependent agencies take on various forms. For example, the Office of Investigations (OI) at the U.S. Department of Agriculture polices not only farm-related federal programs but also the Food Stamp Program.[27] The Customs Service (CS) is charged with administering the Tariff Act of 1930, as well as an array of other acts, among them the Anti-Smuggling Act,[28] Controlled Substances and Export Act,[29] and many others.[30] The CS has arrest powers over individuals who are engaged in practices aimed at circumventing the customs laws; it also enforces import and export restrictions and is engaged in the collection of customs duties.

The Intelligence Division (ID) of the Internal Revenue Service (discussed in chapter 14) polices the tax laws of this country. The Postal Inspection Service (PIS) of the U.S. Postal Service polices the U.S. mails. Crimes within the jurisdiction of PIS include mail frauds, illegal transmission of narcotics, thefts of mail or other postal valuables, bombs sent through the mails, attacks on postal employees or property, and the mailing of prohibited articles. PIS has a staff of over 1500 investigators, and training includes a 16-week course in the use of firearms, legal matters, search-and-seizure techniques, and postal operations.

The closest thing to a national police in this country is the Federal Bureau of Investigation (FBI). Its jurisdiction includes acts of espionage, crimes on government and Indian reservations, violations of civil rights, bribery of federal officials, bankruptcy frauds, bank robberies, crimes on the high seas, and kidnappings. In addition, immigration matters, use of the mails to convey a threat (extortion), interstate transportation of stolen property, the wire fraud statute, and thefts of funds from federally insured institutions would also come within the FBI's jurisdiction.

There is an array of other nonindependent agencies, each employing a large number of investigators and having jurisdiction over specific acts involving the economy. However, these units usually have no subpoena power and must rely on the Justice Department for both civil and criminal prosecution of their cases. For example, U.S. Agriculture Department attorneys do not prosecute violations of laws. Cases are referred to the Justice Department for prosecution. In essence, these units only investigate and refer to the Justice Department cases for either civil or criminal prosecution or both. The decision to prosecute rests with that department.

The independent agencies are based on the Interstate Commerce Commission (ICC) model.[31] This model has a decisionmaking body called the Commission. The latter has executive, legislative, and prosecutorial powers.

Technically, although creatures of the Congress, these regulatory agencies are independent of both the executive and legislative branches of government. The commissioners that head them serve five-year terms; they are nominated by the President and confirmed by the Senate. In creating this model, Congress hoped to insulate these agencies from political pressures. However, the reverse has been the case. As a result of this insulation from external forces, the agencies have fallen captive to the very industries they were established to police and regulate.[32]

These independent agencies have policing divisions within them, usually known as divisions of enforcement. The latter investigate all violations that fall within the jurisdiction of their individual agency and refer all findings to their respective commission. The findings are summarized in a memorandum of recommendation, which lists the facts of the investigation, the recommendations of the investigators, and violations of law. The commission must then decide which one of the following three courses it will pursue: (1) administrative action, (2) criminal referral, and (3) civil prosecution. The commission has the option to pursue all three courses at its discretion.

Administrative action involves a hearing within the agency, with an employee of the agency sitting in judgment. The latter is known as a hearing examiner or administrative trial judge.[33] The agency's own attorneys will prosecute the case, and the respondent (the charged party or corporation) will have its attorneys presenting its defense. Holdings of these administrative tribunals are appealable first to the commission and then to the local U.S. Court of Appeals.

Criminal referrals are recommendations for criminal prosecution by an agency to the Justice Department.[34] These are in the form of a criminal referral memorandum. The facts of the case are outlined, as well as the violations of law. Decisions to prosecute rest with the Justice Department. If it chooses not to prosecute, the agency has no criminal jurisdiction of its own. A U.S. Attorney may occasionally ask the agency to refer the case to his office, thus circumventing the Justice Department. However, even that decision rests with the prosecutor and not the agency.

The agency has the option of conducting a civil prosecution, with its own attorneys prosecuting the case. Unfortunately, the impact of this route is limited. The agency can ask a federal court to order the defendant to cease and desist from further violating the law, and it may ask for monetary damages. To avoid prolonged civil litigation, the agency usually opts for a consent decree. This is an agreement between the agency and the defendant, whereupon the latter agrees not to further violate the law; there is no admission of guilt. If the defendant does violate the agreement, the agency can ask the court to hold him or her in civil contempt. However, this is rare, since the agency does not monitor its consent agreements. Further, the contempt citation requires proof that in fact there was such a violation, and this is no easy task. More than 90 percent of all agency prosecutions culminate in consent decrees.

The independent regulatory agencies have fared no better than the other segments of the federal apparatus in the investigation of white-collar crimes. The federal apparatus has proven receptive to political pressure from powerful interest.[35] Further, the federal apparatus has shown itself unable to move swiftly and decisively against white-collar felons. Most cases never surface but rather die within the agencies—victims of bureaucratic red tape. Only a small percentage of all investigations actually reach prosecution, and these usually take the consent-decree route. Criminal prosecutions are rare and usually culminate with a slap on the wrist.

Presently, the local investigatory apparatus is too fragmented, ill-trained, and lacking in resources to be of any real substantive value in the investigation of complex white-collar crimes. The federal apparatus is too antiquated and riddled with bureaucratic red tape to be of any real value and assistance to the local police forces. Consequently, white-collar felons enjoy de facto immunity from prosecution. Funds, training, and administrative reforms are badly needed to turn the tide in the public's favor.

Notes

1. Eugene L. Meyer, "Deputies Have Right To Be Fat, Ansell Claims," *Washington Post*, November 13, 1977, p. C-1.

2. Leonard Buder, "Detectives Refusal of Cases Is Studied," *New York Times*, October 23, 1977, p. 1.

3. Hazel B. Kerper, *Introduction to the Criminal Justice System* (St. Paul, Minn.: West, 1972), p. 417; see also, Michael J. Kelly, *Police Chief Selection* (Washington, D.C.: Police Foundation, 1975).

4. For a review of police corruption, see Donald R. Cressey, *Theft of the Nation* (New York: Harper & Row, 1969), pp. 248-289; Fred J. Cook, "The People v. the Mob; Or Who Rules New Jersey?" *New York Times Magazine*, February 1, 1970; Robert Daley, "The Cop Who Knew Too Much," *New York Magazine*, March 28, 1977; and Jonathan Rubinstein, *City Police* (New York: Ballantine Books, 1974).

5. William J. Chambliss, "The State and Criminal Law," in *Whose Law What Order*, William J. Chambliss and Milton Mankoff, eds. (New York: Wiley, 1976), p. 75.

6. Ibid., p. 76.

7. Ibid., p. 129.

8. "Hans Gross," in *Pioneers in Criminology*, 2d ed., Herman Mannheim, ed. (Montclair, N.J.: Patterson Smith, 1973), p. 305.

9. For a review of federal agencies, see Victor G. Rosenblum, "Handling Citizen Initiates Complaints: An Introductory Study of Federal Agency Procedures and Practices," *Administrative Law Rev.* (1972):1.

10. National Commission on Law Observance and Enforcement, *Report on Police* (Washington, D.C.: Government Printing Office, 1931), pp. 121-136.

11. The President's Commission on Law Enforcement and the Administration of Justice, *The Challenge of Crime in a Free Society* (Washington, D.C.: Government Printing Office, 1967), p. 119.

12. S. Anthony McCann, *County-Wide Law Enforcement: A Report on a Survey of Central Police Services in 97 Urban Counties* (Washington, D.C.: National Association of Counties, 1975), p. 1.

13. Ibid., p. 7.

14. Ibid., p. 1.

15. See Metropolitan Police Department, *Fiscal Year 1976 Annual Report* (Washington, D.C.: Metropolitan Police Department, 1977), p. 6.

16. Ibid., pp. 43-46; see also, Joseph Fink and Lloyd G. Sealy, *The Community and the Police—Conflict or Cooperation* (New York: Wiley, 1974).

17. A number of large cities have established small consumer fraud units to deal with fraud-related problems that afflict the consuming public. However, these are still small, ill-funded, and lack adequate training.

18. Metropolitan Police Department, *Fiscal Year 1976 Annual Report*, p. 74.

19. Based on my interviews with both police officers and prosecutors within the District of Columbia.

20. Metropolitan Police Department, *Fiscal Year 1976 Annual Report*, pp. 46-47.

21. For a discussion of possible cooperation between local and federal agencies and how this could be accomplished in joint investigations, see Herbert Edelhertz et al., *The Investigation of White Collar Crime* (Washington, D.C.: Government Printing Office, 1977), pp. 47-51.

22. George Lardner, Jr., "Do's, Don'ts of House JFK Probe," *Washington Post*, November 6, 1977, p. A-1.

23. Edward Walsh, "Bell, Carter Divergence on Helms Case Clarified," *Washington Post*, November 3, 1977, p. A-2.

24. Political corruption has seriously tarnished and impaired the investigative capability of many Congressional committees, see "Hill Aide Reported Paid $25,000 by Businessman," *Washington Post*, November 1, 1977, p. A-5.

25. Don Campbell, "Plan to Cut Agencies Slows Down," *Burlington Free Press*, August 25, 1977, p. 1A.

26. For a review of some of these problems, see August Bequai, *Computer Crime* (Lexington, Mass.: Lexington Books, D.C. Heath, 1977).   27. John V. Graziano, "Department of Agriculture: The Third Largest Criminal Investigative Force in Federal Government," *The Police Chief*, July 1975, pp. 54-55.

28. 19 U.S.C., sec. 1701-1711.

29. 21 U.S.C., secs. 843, 951-966.

30. See 31 U.S.C., secs. 1051-1122; 49 U.S.C., sec. 1472; and 18 U.S.C., sec. 25.

31. August Bequai, "White Collar Crime Plea Bargaining," *Trial Magazine*, July 1977, p. 38.

32. For a review of the problems of regulatory agencies, see Bradley Graham, "Public Barely Wins in Agency Hearings," *Washington Post*, August 8, 1977, p. D-110; see also, William H. Jones, "Regulatory Agency Nominees' Quality Hit in Report to Senate," *Washington Post*, February 10, 1977, p. C-1.

33. For a review of administrative agency procedures, see Kenneth C. Davis, *Administrative Law* (St. Paul, Minn.: West, 1972), pp. 219-226.

34. August Bequai, "White Collar Crime Plea Bargaining," pp.40-42.

35. Anthony Sampson, *The Sovereign State of ITT* (New York: Stein & Day, 1973); this book is an excellent profile in corporate corruption.

17 The Problems of Prosecutors

A lengthy investigation has disclosed that U.S. marshals and their deputies in several major cities may have been involved in mob payoffs, extortion, and narcotics trafficking.[1] A number of these individuals were forced to resign. When a key official of the Marshals Service was asked why there had been no prosecutions, he noted that this was up to the U.S. Justice Department. In a large Eastern city, a well-known U.S. Attorney resigned under White House pressure.[2] This official had an excellent record in the area of white-collar crime prosecutions. Not to be outdone, prosecutors in a large Southern city charged that the local U.S. Attorney had dropped a criminal investigation involving a friend of the President of the United States in order to stay in office another year and not jeopardize his government pension.[3]

These examples serve to illustrate the highly political nature of our prosecutorial system. Often, white-collar criminals have access to large sums of money and can influence powerful political officials. Many local prosecutors must be elected, and this process tends to further politicize the system.[4] Federal prosecutors are no exception. They sustain the political process that produced them.[5] Since the end of World War II, the majority of those who held the office of U.S. Attorney General were political figures who played key roles in the election of the President.[6] The office of prosecutor, whether at the local or federal level, also suffers from antiquated approaches and policies in the area of white-collar crime. Many prosecutors, especially at the local level, lack the requisite training and resources to meet the challenge. Whether the present apparatus will meet the future challenge of white-collar crime remains to be seen.

Local Prosecution

Our prosecutorial machinery is divided into two categories: (1) local, and (2) federal. At the local level, the office of prosecutor may take the form of a district attorney, state attorney, county attorney, or attorney general. The latter is usually the statewide prosecutor, with jurisdiction over the entire state. In some states, he may enjoy both civil and criminal jurisdiction, while in others, only civil.[7] The other local prosecutors usually have jurisdiction over a city or county; and in many instances, this jurisdiction involves criminal prosecution. The majority of state and local prosecutors are usually elected officials and are thus responsive to the political pressures of their environments.

District attorneys and county attorneys also suffer from outdated practices, a lack of funds, and poor training. Prosecutors rely on the local police departments to investigate and bring cases to their office for prosecution. At the local level, law enforcement agencies lack such training and the necessary funds to conduct extensive and complex investigations, such as those involving white-collar crimes. Even the larger local prosecutorial offices are poorly prepared for the demands of white-collar crime prosecutions, which are often complex and usually quite difficult to investigate and prosecute. Most jurisdictions have neither the money nor the manpower to pursue such cases.

A study of 41 local prosecutorial offices found that in 1975 all these offices combined assigned only 149 attorneys to prosecute white-collar crime cases; they were assisted by 147 investigators, 89 paralegals, and 69 volunteers.[8] In one year alone, this group had to handle more than 100,000 complaints and inquiries.[9] A 1976 study of various local prosecutorial offices found that the vast majority of these allocated few resources, in terms of both manpower and funds, to white-collar crime cases.[10] Akron, Ohio, with a population of more than 500,000, allocated one attorney, six investigators, one secretary, and a paralegal to its consumer fraud unit. The city of Baltimore allocated three attorneys, six investigators, two secretaries, and two law clerks. Boston, with a population of over 700,000, assigned only one attorney to prosecute fraud cases; Buffalo, New York, with a population of more than 1 million, assigned only two attorneys; Chicago assigned only six attorneys and a support staff of 16 investigators, secretaries, and paralegals. The entire state of Connecticut assigned only two attorneys and three investigators; while Dallas, Texas, with a population of 1,327,000, had no full-time attorneys assigned to white-collar crime cases. On the average, the largest local prosecutorial offices in this nation assigned fewer than six attorneys to prosecute white-collar crime cases.

At the state level, a survey of state attorney general offices disclosed that only 30 of these state prosecutors had consumer fraud units.[11] Only 40 state prosecutors had budgets in excess of $1 million annually, while three jurisdictions had budgets of under $500,000.[12] When one considers that some white-collar crime prosecutions can easily exceed the $1 million mark, the lack of monetary (in addition to manpower) resources at the local level becomes apparent. Some of these offices have received grants, but these awards have ranged from less than $1000 to $1.6 million.[13] It should also be pointed out that the grants were not solely for white-collar crime prosecutions, but for a myriad of other law enforcement-related areas. Further, the number of attorneys employed by all the state prosecutors combined is less than 7,000.[14] The majority of these offices employ fewer than 100 full-time attorneys.[15]

The prosecutorial machinery at the local, county, city, and state levels is too small, ill-equipped, and politicized to act decisively against major white-collar crime cases. When prosecutions have taken place, they usually involved minor cases. This is not to say that local prosecutors cannot play an important role. They must do so; but before this occurs, much is required. Training, funding, and a sense of professionalism are badly needed to bring this machinery in line with the demands of present criminology. In addition, greater cooperation between these local prosecutors is also needed.

Federal Prosecutors

The chief federal prosecutor is the U.S. Attorney General. He directs the U.S. Justice Department and its panoply of divisions and branches, with over 94 United States Attorneys. The office of Attorney General is as old as the Republic itself. It was first established in 1789 to both advise the President and his cabinet on matters relating to law and direct the prosecution of federal crimes. The system of United States Attorneys is also as old as the Republic; and from the beginning, these local federal prosecutors were political creatures, responsive to the needs and whims of local political powers.[16] After each was elected, Presidents Truman, Kennedy, and Nixon all appointed their campaign managers to the post of Attorney General.

Until 1853 the Attorney General was only a part-time employee of the federal apparatus. He paid many of the expenses of that office out of his own pocket. The Justice Department itself was formally established in 1870; and as late as 1887, the United States Supreme Court, in the now classic case of *United States* v. *San Jacinto Tin Company,* warned that the political nature of that office could pose a threat to the rights of the citizenry.[17] Watergate was to prove the Court correct.

In 1924 the Teapot Dome Scandal broke, and the Senate called for the removal of the Justice Department from the political arena. The American Bar Association has also called for legislation that would remove the federal prosecutorial machinery from the political arena.[18] One former U.S. attorney has noted that:

Loyalty to the political interest of the administration often requires disloyalty to the goal of impartial justice. . . . It is not enough to change the label on the Department of Justice. What must be done is to change the functions of the Attorney General up and down the line.[19]

The Nixon era corroborated this statement. Nevertheless, the office of Attorney General continues to be highly politicized.

The Justice Department itself is a myriad of divisions, bureaus, and branches. It employs more than 50,000 individuals and has an annual budget of over $2 billion. For purposes of white-collar crime prosecutions, the key divisions within the Department are those of Antitrust, Tax, and Criminal. Each is headed by an Assistant Attorney General. The Antitrust Division deals with violations of law affecting the free marketplace.[20] The Tax Division handles all prosecutions involving violations of our tax laws—this includes both civil and criminal litigation.[21] The most important of these divisions is probably the Criminal, which is composed of eight sections.[22] Of these, the fraud, organized crime, and general crimes sections are of prime importance. The Criminal Division operates to a large extent as a clearinghouse, referring key white-collar cases to the U.S. Attorney's offices for criminal prosecution. On rare occasions, attorneys from this division go directly to the field to prosecute their own cases.

The workhorse of the federal prosecutorial machinery, with the exception of such specialized units as the Tax and Antitrust Divisions, is the local federal prosecutor—the U.S. Attorney. The total number of attorneys employed by these 94 offices is less than 2000. The larger offices are those of the District of Columbia, Southern District of New York, Central District of California, and Northern District of Illinois. The largest office employs about 160 attorneys, while the smallest office employs less than a dozen. Most of these offices, with the exception of the few larger ones, have no specialized units to handle white-collar crime cases.[23]

White-collar crime units are usually called "fraud sections." On the average, they employ about eight attorneys, plus a small staff of secretaries and paralegals. At present, only the U.S. Attorney for the Southern District of New York, and his counterpart in Newark, New Jersey, employ any investigators. The other local federal prosecutors rely on the federal investigative apparatus for their referrals. The combined manpower of these local federal fraud sections does not exceed 200 attorneys. It is this small core of federal prosecutors that handles the bulk of all federal prosecutions involving white-collar crimes. In essence, they are asked to do a Herculean task, which is far beyond the resources and manpower at their disposal.

The federal apparatus employs more than 10,000 lawyers; the Justice Department alone employs over 1000, excluding the attorneys found in the 94 U.S. Attorney offices. However, of this large reservoir of legal talent, white-collar prosecution rests on the shoulders of fewer than 200 assistant U.S. Attorneys (the fraud sections). There are some exceptions, such as the special task groups that operate out of Washington, D.C. and some of the regional organized crime strike forces. However, even if this additional pool of prosecutors is added to that of the local fraud sections, the total number would still be only a small percentage of the entire federal legal reservoir.

Many U.S. Attorneys justify their need to exert total control over the prosecution of federal white-collar crime cases because the bulk of the federal legal force generally lacks training in this area. However, a recent U.S. Senate staff study has found that a sizable majority of all federal judges feel that local federal prosecutors also lack experience and training.[24] The justification for such control is really political. Local powerful political groups maintain tight control over local federal prosecution by simply exerting control over the selection and operation of their U.S. Attorney offices. They guard with jealousy their local prerogatives, and oppose any change in the present local federal prosecutorial machinery.

As a result, at present we have a massive federal prosecutorial apparatus that spends most of its time "shuffling paper." Trial work is handled only by a small number of assistant U.S. Attorneys and a small number of specialized units that operate out of the Justice Department in Washington. The bulk of the federal legal force reviews memos and writes interoffice opinions. Internal Revenue Service attorneys and those of other specialized agencies must defer prosecution to generalists who work out of local federal prosecutorial offices. The federal machinery employs a large body of legal talent; the Justice Department is the largest prosecutorial body in the world; and resources and manpower are not lacking. In large part, white-collar crime prosecutions have been hampered by bureaucratic red tape, absence of a firm commitment; the politicized nature of the present U.S. Attorney offices, and a hesitancy to shift prosecutorial strategies. The entire federal prosecutorial apparatus is in need of review and revision.

The Federal Arsenal

On occasion, prosecutors complain that they are handicapped by a lack of requisite legal tools to deal effectively with white-collar crimes. At the local level, there is some merit to this assertion. Many localities still cling to the old common law. Few have passed any legislation in the area of commercial frauds. However, the situation is quite different at the federal level. The problem here is not a dearth of laws but rather a labyrinth of legal statutes that often confuse and intimidate the federal prosecutor. The federal code needs streamlining, not the addition of more laws and regulations. Presently, there exists a sufficient number of federal laws to imprison our entire adult population. The answer is not more money and manpower but rather a better utilization of present resources. The bureaucracies (the Justice Department and U.S. Attorney offices included) are reluctant to embark upon this move toward efficiency. There is a vested interest in preserving the status quo.

There are numerous federal statutes that can be, and have been, employed in the prosecution of white-collar crimes. For example, the wire fraud statute makes it a crime to use the wires, radio, telegram, or television in interstate or foreign commerce for purposes of furthering a fraudulent scheme.[25] The mail fraud statutes make it a felony to use the mails for "obtaining money or property by means of false or fraudulent pretenses."[26] A federal official who embezzles public funds can be fined and/or imprisoned for his act.[27] A federal official "charged with the duty of keeping accounts of any kind" can be imprisoned if he alters or falsifies them.[28] Schemes to defraud federally insured institutions can likewise result in fines and prison sentences.[29]

There are also an array of other federal statutes that address the problem of securities and commodities frauds. There are numerous laws and regulations that govern programs related to health, education, welfare, and agriculture. The problem, clearly, is not an absence of rules and regulations but rather an "indigestion" of laws. There is simply too much, scattered in too many texts. In order to meet the needs of society and to protect the rights of the individual, we need to simplify this legal maze. Review and reform of the present federal penal code should be a top priority. Prosecutors do not need more laws; they have the requisite legal arsenal. What is currently needed is the will and strategy to apply it effectively.

Notes

1. Tom Renner, "U.S. Investigating Corruption in Marshalls Service," *Washington Post,* September 12, 1977, pp. A-1, A-7.

2. Stuart Auerbach, "U.S. Attorney in N.J. Resigns, Assails President," *Washington Post,* September 13, 1977, p. A-7.

3. Robert G. Kaiser, "Pension Called Motive in Lance Probe Halt," *Washington Post,* September 15, 1977, pp. A-1, A-12.

4. See Paul B. Weston and Kenneth M. Wells, *The Administration of Justice* (Englewoods, N.J.: Prentice-Hall, 1967), pp. 8, 9; for a review of attempts to depoliticize the office of prosecutor, see American Bar Association Project on Standards for Criminal Justice, *Standards Relating to the Prosecution and Defense Function* (Chicago, Ill.: American Bar Association, 1970), pp. 48-100.

5. Stuart Auerbach, "U.S. Attorney in N.J. Resigns, Assails President," p. A-7.

6. American Bar Association Project on Standards for Criminal Justice, *Standards Relating to the Prosecution and Defense Function,* pp. 7, 8.

7. In the state of New York, the attorney general has only civil jurisdiction; all criminal cases are referred to local prosecutors, such as district attorneys, for action.

8. Economic Crime Project of the National District Attorneys Association, *Fighting the $40 Billion Rip-Off* (Chicago, Ill.: National District Attorneys Association, 1976), pp. 5, 6.

9. Ibid., p. 6.

10. For a review of these offices, see ibid., pp. 12-45.

11. National Association of Attorneys General, *Selected Statistics on the Office of Attorney General* (Raleigh, N.C.: National Association of Attorneys General, 1975), p. 1.

12. Ibid., p. 17.

13. Ibid., p. 25.

14. Ibid., p. 40.

15. Ibid.

16. American Bar Association Project on Standards for Criminal Justice, *Standards Relating to the Prosecution and Defense Function,* pp. 8, 9, 23.

17. 125 U.S. 278 (1887).

18. American Bar Association Project on Standards for Criminal Justice, *Standards Relating to the Prosecution and Defense Function,* pp. 8, 9.

19. For examples of abuses at the federal prosecutorial level, read Robert A. Hutchison, *Vesco* (New York: Praeger, 1974), p. 368.

20. U.S. Justice Department, *Annual Report of the Attorney General of the United States for 1975* (Washington, D.C.: Government Printing Office, 1976), p. 111.

21. Ibid., p. 135.

22. Ibid., p. 91.

23. Based on my own personal experience as a trial attorney with the Securities and Exchange Commission; I was surprised on a number of occasions to find that local federal prosecutors did not know that trading on inside information and other securities-related irregularities were illegal.

24. Richard E. Cohen, "Justice Reports" *National Journal* (April 21, 1973):16.

25. 18 U.S.C., sec. 1343.

26. 18 U.S.C., secs. 1341, 1342.

27. 18 U.S.C., secs. 641, 643.

28. 18 U.S.C., sec. 2073.

29. 18 U.S.C., secs. 1001-1027.

18 Litigation Problems

One of the nation's largest auto makers, under investigation by the federal government for alleged tax violations, has charged that the Internal Revenue Service (IRS) has acted improperly in its investigation.[1] Company officials allege that IRS agents abused and violated the constitutional rights of company officials. In another case, the Federal Communications Commission (FCC) revoked the license of a North Carolina radio station.[2] FCC investigators charged that the station had overbilled more than 100 of its advertising accounts by more than $60,000. In another government investigation, the Federal Bureau of Investigation (FBI) employed hidden electronic listening devices to monitor the meeting of four individuals.[3] One major national newspaper called it an "Orwellian act."

The investigation of white-collar crimes is no easy task. Investigators are handicapped by poor training, an antiquated investigatorial apparatus, and procedural safeguards that have not been well defined in this area. There is no "stop and frisk" in white-collar crime cases; there are no automobile searches; search warrants are rarely employed; investigatory detentions are not used. The world of the white-collar crime policeman is something alien to the average citizen, an area where criminal procedure is not well defined. Consequently, both the investigator and investigated operate in a large, uncharted sea.

Historical Development of Procedural Safeguards

If one were to ask the average citizen what an arrest was, a fairly coherent answer would probably be provided. Yet, if one were to ask the average jurist what an administrative subpoena was, few would be able to describe it. The average policeman knows what the adequate grounds are for an arrest; custodial situations, however, take on a different meaning within the white-collar crime arena. Investigators in this arena wear no uniforms; few, in fact, even carry guns. It is a paper war; lost and won by the ability of government agents to follow the paper trail.

Much of our criminal procedure, and related safeguards, has its roots in seventeenth century England. Her monarchs, in an attempt to quash opposition, created the dreaded Star Chamber court; all those suspected of treason against the crown were ordered to appear before it. General warrants were issued at the discretion of the executing officer to ensure the appearance of suspects. In 1765 the now classic case of *Entick* v. *Carrington* came before the courts; the judiciary held that government agents, empowered with a warrant, who had seized the plaintiff's books and records were liable to him in damages for trespass.[4] The court noted that the individual's interest in being free from compelled self-incrimination extended to his books and records.

The early twentieth century, however, saw the rise of various federal and local agencies charged with policing and regulating various sectors of the economy. This new class of policemen, however, took the courts by surprise. Their modus operandi differed somewhat from that of the traditional police forces. These agencies employed administrative subpoenas to gather their evidence, and records played a key role in their investigations. Further, many of these agencies had been empowered by their legislatures to make on-sight inspections and examinations of records.

The judiciary, schooled under the common law, was at first reluctant to allow these new agencies powers clearly denied the old police forces. For example, in 1908 the U.S. Supreme Court held that the Interstate Commerce Commission had no power to compel witnesses to testify.[5] Several years later, another federal agency, investigating violations of its jurisdiction, was also frustrated when it attempted to subpoena books and records from one of the parties involved in its investigation.[6] The court noted that the agency had not shown that probable cause existed to indicate a violation of law. The courts, both federal and local, were reluctant to allow these new policing bodies powers they had denied the traditional police forces. However, traditional police work alone would not suffice in the white-collar crime arena. In the early 1950s courts began to acknowledge that these new policing bodies had the right to conduct investigations and subpoena witnesses and documents when necessary to ensure that "corporate behavior" was consistent with the law.[7]

Powers of the New Policing Bodies

The 1960s saw an active U.S. Supreme Court; numerous decisions were handed down, further clarifying the rights of individuals under police investigation. For example, the now classic *Miranda* case made note of the subtle dangers posed by custodial interrogation.[8] The U.S. Supreme Court outlined four key points in *Miranda:* (1) a suspect has the right to remain silent, (2) anything he says may be used against him, (3) he has the right to counsel, and (4) if unable to obtain counsel of his own choosing because of financial difficulties, counsel will be appointed to represent him. A waiver of these rights must be voluntary. Numerous other court decisions have also dealt with the rights of suspects under custody.[9]

However, although numerous courts, both local and federal, have dealt with the rights of suspects and the area of investigations, few have addressed themselves to the area of white-collar crime investigatory police work. In large part, this is due to the fact that few white-collar crime investigations result in criminal prosecution. The majority never surface at all. Of those which do, more than 90 percent are resolved civilly via the consent-decree route. In addition, investigations involving white-collar crimes are usually confidential. Whereas the public knows the names of suspects in bank robberies, the names of suspects in stock frauds are rarely made public. Even when the case finally surfaces in a court of law, it is usually weakened and restrained. Presently, the Federal Trade Commission (FTC) is weighing whether to make public the names of companies and individuals involved in its formal investigations.[10]

Criminal procedure in the white-collar crime area is further muddled by the fact that many of these crimes are not only handled civilly but may (and usually do) involve both civil and criminal violations. It is difficult to divide the two; consequently, many cases are finally determined in the civil arena. Agencies like the FTC, ICC, and the other local and federal regulatory bodies have the power to initiate investigations; they can also issue administrative subpoenas, once those investigations are formal. They can also bring civil suit or refer the matter for criminal prosecution to the Justice Department, in the case of a federal agency. In the case of a local investigatory body, they can refer it to a district attorney for prosecution.

Initially, investigations by these new policing bodies differ little from those of any detective bureau in a large metropolitan area of the United States. Once an indication of some violation comes to the attention of these agencies, they either contact the individuals involved and ask for a field interview or call the parties to the agency's offices. At the IRS, for example, once an agent receives information that may involve a tax law violation, the party is called to the IRS offices for an office audit or a field audit is initiated. The pattern is essentially the same at other agencies.

These policing agencies also have the power to conduct regulatory or administrative searches. Since many of the agencies have noncriminal policing roles, regulatory searches (such as those involving health codes, safety violations, banking areas, etc.) are usually allowed by the courts without the need for a search warrant. Courts have taken the position that these searches are civil in nature, and criminal sanctions come into play only after the violator has refused to take steps to remedy the violations found on his premise. For example, the Securities and Exchange Commission usually conducts visits to various brokerage firms around the country. Violations are usually handled in a noncriminal manner.

The U.S. Supreme Court has upheld such searches. For example, in *United States* v. *Biswell,* federal agents visited a pawnshop licensed under the federal gun control legislation.[11] They found weapons the defendant was not licensed to possess. The defense challenged the search as having been made without a warrant. The Court, however, found the search had been proper and within the requirements of the federal legislation. There have been cases, however, that have successfully challenged these administrative searches.[12] The visitation rights exercised by the regulatory agencies may, at times, be fishing expeditions indeed. They may have as their objective criminal prosecution, although this is contrary to the spirit of the legislation that empowered them.[13] Thus, through the simple device of an administrative search, the regulatory agency may be evading the need for a warrant. This entire area is one that has yet to be dealt with adequately by the courts. Since the agencies wear two hats—civil and criminal—it is difficult to discern which hat they are wearing at the time of their visit. It places the burden on the defendant to prove that in fact their original intent was to develop a criminal case through a civil vehicle.

Defendants have often charged that the agencies have employed administrative subpoenas to develop criminal cases. More recently, the IRS and the SEC have come under such attacks. These agencies have power to issue administrative subpoenas; if the person to whom the summons is issued fails to comply with it, he can be fined and/or imprisoned. Courts have upheld these subpoenas, even if they are likely to produce evidence that may be used in a criminal prosecution.[14] Often these subpoenas may be employed to aid a sister agency that has no such power; the information obtained is then made available to other agencies. The defendant obviously faces the difficult task of trying to prove that in fact the intent of the subpoena was to conduct a criminal fishing expedition under the guise of a civil action. These can be extremely difficult to prove. The problem here, as with the regulatory searches, lies in the dual role of these agencies—they investigate both civil and criminal violations. Many times the dividing line between the two is not clearly defined.

Often, in their investigations, the agency investigators come across material that may fall within the attorney-client privilege. This rule has its roots in the common law. Under it, all communications between an attorney and his client are privileged; the privilege may not be asserted or waived by the attorney. The purpose of the rule is to promote free discourse between an attorney and his client. The rule, however, is composed of four elements: (1) only the client can claim the privilege, (2) the communication must have been made to an attorney, (3) in the course of legal services, and (4) the communication must be by word or act. If the communication is divulged to a third person by the client or, pursuant to his instructions, by counsel, then the privilege is waived.[15] If the communication relates to a joint venture in which both counsel and his client are involved, the privilege is waived.[16] Since, in many white-collar frauds, attorneys may be direct participants in these ventures, communications between them and the other participants in the fraud sometimes find protection under this rule.

Communications between an accountant and his client are not privileged at the federal level, nor are the workpapers of an accountant privileged at the federal level. However, many states have enacted legislation that does establish an accountant-client privilege; and in a local court, such a privilege might be raised against a state regulatory body. Additionally, there are no broker-client privileges; and, therefore, communications between the two are not privileged.

Some of the federal agencies have also made use of the Omnibus Crime Control and Safe Streets Act of 1968 as an investigatory tool.[17] The act prohibits any individual from intercepting any wire or oral communication by the use of any electronic, mechanical, or other device, except as provided in the act. A court can authorize electronic interception if it finds that there is probable cause to believe that a felony has been or is about to be committed, and that normal investigative procedures have been attempted and have failed. The court, however, must also specify the nature, location, and description of the facilities in which the communications will be intercepted, the particular conversation sought, and the period during which the interception is authorized. With the growing sophistication of technology, the act can prove an effective weapon in the area of white-collar crime if properly employed.

The new policing agencies have assumed an increasingly important role in the area of white-collar fraud investigations. With increased attention to this area of crime, their roles will have to be better defined. Present criminal procedures tend to be vague and inconsistent in this area; the courts and legislatures have concentrated on traditional policing and have allowed these large investigative bodies to establish their own internal rules and procedures. In many instances, these fail to address themselves to the needs of a criminal investigation. Often, defendants do not know if they are the targets of a civil or criminal inquiry; defense attorneys often "do not know where their clients stand." The IRS, for example, has designated its Intelligence Division as its sole criminal investigatory organ. This is not the case with many of the other agencies. As a result, confusion permeates this entire area.

Constitutional Protections in Investigations

A number of constitutional rights, widely applied in traditional police investigations, could also easily be adapted to the white-collar crime arena. The Fourth Amendment of the U.S. Constitution protects every individual against unreasonable searches of his person, house, office, or vehicle, including his papers and effects. This amendment also provides that no warrants will be issued unless upon probable cause, supported by oath, and describing the place to be searched and the person or things to be seized. Warrants are rarely employed in white-collar crime investigations. In large part, there are three reasons for this: (1) the regulatory agencies rely on their administrative subpoenas and visitation rights when possible; (2) since these cases are usually complex, it is difficult to specify with certainty the place to be searched and the things to be seized; and (3) many of the targets of these investigations tend to be professionals and businessmen, thus producing a reluctance to employ warrants because of the social stigma they tend to carry. One investigator candidly admitted, "we cannot treat them like common thieves." However, with increasing prosecutions in this area, greater use of this amendment is expected.

The Fifth Amendment prohibits compelling any individual to be a witness against himself in a criminal case; the amendment applies only to federal procedure; but its privileges against self-incrimination has been incorporated into the due process clause of the Fourteenth Amendment, making it applicable also to the states. A witness in a white-collar crime investigation may be called by federal agents and interviewed. He has, however, the right to claim the privilege if answers may tend to incriminate him. Federal agents tend, at least in cases which may have criminal consequences, to advise the witness of his right against self-incrimination. The mere claim of the privilege is not a right in and of itself to refuse to answer questions; it must appear that the answers constitute a dangerous disclosure that may lead to incriminating evidence. There is a mistaken belief on the part of many witnesses, and also their attorneys, that federal agencies can grant immunity from prosecution. As a result, on several occasions witnesses have mistakenly made self-incriminating disclosures.

The privilege, however, does not bar the government from requesting an individual to give handwriting samples; in fraud cases, these can be of immense value to investigators.[18] The individual can also be asked to give blood samples, as well as samples of his voice. The privilege does not protect the custodian of a corporation from producing the corporate books and records, even if these would serve to incriminate the corporation as well as himself. The amendment is not available to corporations as a defense; as creatures of the state, they are open to inspection and examination by government agents. However, if an individual is asked questions about his own private papers, he can refuse to answer based on his Fifth Amendment privilege against self-incrimination.

The Sixth Amendment guarantees an individual the right to counsel in criminal proceedings. Many regulatory agencies have adopted their own internal rules. For example, Rule 7(b) of the SEC's Rules of Practice provides each witness in an investigation the right to counsel. In criminal cases, an indigent defendant is provided with counsel. The right arises whenever an individual is taken into custody or otherwise deprived of his freedom.[19] The problem in white-collar crime investigations is the term *custody;* it is employed with traditional police measures in mind. It has little relevance in fraud cases; there suspects are rarely taken into custody and have their first contact with the criminal process usually at the indictment stage.

Evidence obtained in an illegal fashion (in violation of any Constitutional provision) will be excluded under the Exclusionary Rule.[20] This "illegal fruits" doctrine relates to evidence, and has been employed with increasing frequency by defense attorneys in white-collar crime prosecutions. If the prosecutor can show that the evidence would have been discovered in any event, courts may allow it in a trial. Only the victim himself can raise the rule as a defense; it cannot be raised by another defendant as a defense. The objective of the rule is to ensure that the police and prosecutors follow proper legal procedures.

The rule could conceivably pose problems in white-collar crime prosecutions. The jurisdictions of the regulatory agencies encompass both civil and criminal areas. Many times, subpoenas and visitation rights are used to develop criminal cases, contrary to the spirit of the legislation that established these agencies. In addition, many of these policing bodies are entering new areas. The courts have concentrated too long on the traditional police concepts. Case law in the fraud area is still in its infancy, and its course remains to be seen.

Notes

1. "Treated Like Gangsters, GM Says of Fraud Probe," *Washington Post,* June 22, 1977, p. D-9.

2. "FCC Takes License of Carolina Station, Cites Billing Fraud," *Wall Street Journal,* August 5, 1977, p. 4.

3. David P. Hodges, "Electronic Visual Surveillance and the Fourth Amendment: The Arrival of Big Brother," *Hastings Constitutional Law Quarterly* III (Winter 1976):261.

4. 19 How. St. Tr., 1029 (1765).

5. *Harriman* v. *Interstate Commerce Commission,* 211 U.S. 407 (1908).

6. *Federal Trade Commission* v. *American Tobacco Company,* 254 U.S. 298 (1924).

7. *United States* v. *Morton Salt Company,* 338 U.S. 632 (1950).

8. *Miranda* v. *Arizona,* 384 U.S. 436 (1966).

9. *Massiah* v. *United States,* 377 U.S. 201 (1964); and *Escobedo* v. *Illinois,* 378 U.S. 478 (1964).

10. "FTC Adopts Two Rules to Speed Up Cases on Unfair Practices," *Wall Street Journal,* February 21, 1975, p. 16.

11. *United States* v. *Biswell*, 406. U.S. 311 (1972).

12. *United States* v. *Wohler*, 382 F.Supp. 229 (1973); and also *United States* v. *Dickerson*, 413 F.2d 1111 (1969).

13. *Federal Trade Commission* v. *American Tobacco Company*, p. 211.

14. *Resiman* v. *Caplin*, 375 U.S. 440 (1964).

15. *Murray* v. *Baldwin*, 43 B.T.A. (1940).

16. *United States* v. *Finley*, 434 F.2d 596 (1970).

17. 18 U.S.C., sec. 2510.

18. *Schmerber* v. *California*, 384 U.S. 757 (1966).

19. *Argersinger* v. *Hamlin*, 407 U.S. 25 (1972).

20. *Knoll Associates, Incorporated* v. *Federal Trade Commission*, 397 F.2d 530 (1968).

19 What the Future Holds in White-Collar Crime

It is Monday morning in Suburbia, U.S.A. Mr.Smith prepares to eat his breakfast, when his wife reminds him to pay the monthly bills. "I thought you paid them last Friday," He responds. "I forgot," is her reply. "I'll take care of them before I leave for work, but please tell me in advance next time." After finishing breakfast, Mr. Smith heads for the touch phone in the living room. He reviews the bills and dials his bank's computer. He proceeds to give a secret code and instructs the computer to transfer funds from his account to that of his creditors. Electronically, and in a matter of minutes, he has paid all his monthly bills. Should his account fall short, the bank's computer will automatically lend Mr. Smith the needed funds, up to a predetermined sum, deducting payments and interest charges as they are due.

Detective McGinnis walks into his office. He works for one of the large metropolitan police forces on the West Coast. He heads for the coffee machine, when his captain asks him to step into his office. "We've had another one," the captain informs him. "How bad was it," asks McGinnis. "Several million dollars. Someone transferred the funds from the LTB account to an East Coast account. We don't know who did it. To make things worse, the funds were then transferred to England. I want you and Tom to get on it right away."

The preceding serves to illustrate the problem of crime in the cashless society or the world of computerized transference of funds. That future is almost upon us. For example, one large food chain in the Washington, D.C. metropolitan area recently announced plans to computerize its checkout operations; optical scanners and computerized point-of-sale terminals would be installed in its stores.[1] Similarly, the nation's largest retail chain announced that it had entered into an agreement to computerize many of its sales transactions, thus further eliminating the need for cash transactions.[2] On the international scale, more than 50 U.S. and Canadian banks have agreed to join a high-speed telecommunications network that is designed to radically speed up the transference of international payment transactions.[3] For an initial fee and monthly charge, member institutions of the Society for Worldwide Interbank Financial Telecommunications (SWIFT), as the system is known, can transmit payment messages through a computerized operation linking several continents. Previously, such fund transfers were conducted either through the mails or Telex. It is estimated that this system will handle more than 100,000 daily messages within the near future.

Defining the Cashless Society

At present there are more than 13,000 commercial banks, with more than 17,000 branches and 248 clearing houses, and 12 Federal Reserve Banks, with their 24 branches, that act as processing points for our present check system.[4] The annual check volume has grown from 5 billion in the 1940s to over 20 billion at present. The entire financial industry is currently suffering from a serious paper glut. Many in the financial industry and others in the business world have come to see the computer as a possible answer to this dilemma.[5] In large part, computer technology can help reduce this glut. The computer can enable bankers to transfer funds, electronically, in a matter of minutes.[6] The system is known as the Electronic Funds Transfer System (EFTS). Plans are now being developed, and implemented, to make EFTS both a domestic and international reality in the near future.

EFTS has been defined as the transmission of data regarding fund transfers over communication networks. The process begins with an input at a computer terminal and culminates in a bookkeeping transaction at a computer center. It may involve the transfer of funds from the account of a buyer to that of the seller, an employer to that of an employee, or between two or more financial institutions, domestically or internationally. Presently, such transactions are conducted with the aid of the mails or cables.

The EFTS offers more than mere speed and reduction of paper work. As an example, a small store could easily accommodate such a system. One or more terminals could be installed within its premises; these would be connected to one or more bank computers. Buyers could be issued identification cards to be used in making purchases at the store. After making a purchase, the buyer could hand his identification card to the clerk who would then insert the card into a reading device. This machine would, in turn, extract information contained on the card (perhaps a magnetic strip located on the back of the card). The clerk would then enter the amount and type of transaction into a communications device connected to the bank's computer. The computer would process the information and effect the transfer of funds from the buyer's account to that of the store. An employer's payroll could also be totally integrated within EFTS. The employer's computer could be programmed to deposit an employee's pay in his or her account.

The requisite technology exists, and the needed foundations have already been laid. For example, in the early 1970s a number of automated clearing houses (ACHs) first began to appear on the West Coast. The ACHs are widely used for the distribution of payroll payments. An employee's salary is encoded on magnetic tapes or punch cards, which are delivered to a local Federal Reserve or its branch. The employer's bank then pays the employee's bank by an interbank settlement at the Federal Reserve Bank. All the information regarding the entire transfer is contained on magnetic tapes or punch cards.

Another key development in this area is the point-of-sale system (POS). This is a more advanced form of electronic funds transference than the ACH, and a further step in the direction of a national EFTS. Under a POS, transactions can be effected without the use of any currency. It is a true cashless system. The buyer presents a store's clerk with an identification card, which the clerk inserts into a terminal. This is one of many terminals that are connected to a bank's computer so that withdrawals and deposits can be made electronically. Such a system is currently operational in a number of states.[7]

Support for Such a System

In addition to the need to deal effectively with the problem of a growing paper glut, a number of reasons have been advanced in support of EFTS. The system may do away with traditional forms of crime. For example, if there is no cash, then armed robberies and various forms of larceny may become a thing of the past. Burglary, too, may decrease, since a fence would have a difficult time evading prosecution—all transactions would be recorded by a bank's computer, available for the authorities to find and review. Additionally, even payoffs and kickbacks could become obsolete, since law enforcement could easily check out the computerized accounts of those under investigation.

Supporters also point out that the elderly, who are presently the targets of traditional felons, would bank and pay all their bills through the convenience of a telephone, thus avoiding the dangerous situations that produce robberies. The infirm could also pay all their bills and conduct their financial transactions from the comfort of their homes. The average consumer would pay his bills from the convenience of his home or office. There are many advantages to having an EFTS, and traditional crime will certainly be affected. Conversely, however, the system could change white-collar crime, make it more difficult to detect and prosecute. Since the workhorse of this cashless system will be the computer, a network of hundreds of thousands of computers connected by millions of feet of cables and terminals would be extremely difficult to police. Further, such a system would facilitate the actions of white-collar criminals unless proper safeguards were taken.

The Rise of New White-Collar Crime

Privacy-related crimes will inevitably grow under EFTS.[8] Voluminous and important data on both individuals and corporations will be stored in computers under EFTS. The data may outline highly confidential material regarding both individuals and firms. Such data could be of value to blackmailers, business competitors, political opponents, credit companies, and even political extremists. A black market could easily emerge and flourish as the result of such data. Valuable information and trade secrets, as well as sensitive information regarding important individuals (for example, a political leader), could be worth millions of dollars to interested parties. As an example, one firm recently paid several million dollars for the preferred customer list of a national book publisher.

The falsification and manipulation of corporate records could easily grow under EFTS. At present, paper trails place certain limitations on this; but in an EFTS, it would be much easier to fabricate corporate assets.[9] Further, payments for nonexistent services, as well as embezzlement, could be expected to grow. With the assistance of insiders who have access to a bank's computer, criminals could easily create false accounts and fabricate transactions, thus misleading both the unsuspecting private sector and police agencies.

With equal ease, computerization could assist the stock manipulator. Fictitious stock buyers and sellers could be created by simply pushing buttons, assets and earnings could be fabricated, and funds could be transferred internationally within a matter of minutes, making recovery difficult, if not impossible. Antitrust problems could also grow, particularly from the system itself.[10] For example, who is to have access to EFTS? Will the large banks squeeze out their smaller competitors?

Embezzlement and pilferage will also take on new forms. With the assistance of a vast system of computers, both insiders and those with access to a terminal will be able to effect transfers of funds, supplies, and materials. Fraud by identification card will also grow, and an entire new industry involving such cards may develop. Credit card fraud will take on a new form and a new target—the EFTS itself. It will be difficult to ensure security in a system composed of large numbers of computers and diversified security measures. Currently, security in the computer area has been shown to be lax; felons have had little, if any, difficulty in penetrating present systems.

Consumer fraud will invariably grow and become more difficult to prosecute. At present a consumer has the option of directing his bank to stop payment on a check if he or she suspects that the transaction may be a fraud. Under EFTS, though, such options will no longer be available to consumers. Funds will be transferred from his account to that of the felon within a matter of minutes. Presently, the consumer has a cancelled check as proof of payments; with it, he can bring either civil action or offer it to the prosecutor as proof of his loss. Under EFTS, there will be no cancelled checks; the problem for prosecutors to resolve will be how to prove that in fact payment was made. In addition, if the funds are transferred to a foreign account, then obtaining even computerized records from a foreign bank may pose a problem, since domestic subpoenas have no jurisdiction abroad. Consumer fraud will be fraught with problems for investigators and prosecutors alike under EFTS.

Computer crime should be expected to grow dramatically, and the computer itself will come under increasing attack. Wiretapping of telephone or other communication lines connected to computers or computer terminals should increase under EFTS. Illegal taps may be employed to intercept and record valuable data. Bugging of computer facilities may also increase, and thus provide felons and other interested elements with valuable data regarding firms and individuals. Various forms of illegal entry into the system could be expected to increase. For example, unauthorized terminals may be employed on a growing scale. Numerous other, more sophisticated forms of electronic penetration will also emerge. Predictably, the computer will come under increasing attack by a growing arsenal of electronic intercepting tools.

EFTS may also open the individual to abuse from the federal bureaucracy. The Bank Secrecy Act of 1970, for example, requires the maintenance of records and the reporting of financial transactions to the government by certain individuals and financial institutions.[11] Originally, the act was passed with the objective of ensuring that organized crime figures not maintain secret foreign bank accounts. In an EFTS environment, the act could play a role, if properly employed, against organized criminal elements. However, a bureaucracy that is not sensitive to the constitutional rights of the individuals could abuse it. The Nixon administration demonstrated this more clearly than mere predictions could ever do.

Policing EFTS

The modern legal armament will undoubtedly prove inadequate to bring EFTS criminals to prosecution. For example, the mail fraud statutes presently pose a formidable weapon in the prosecutor's arsenal.[12] However, in the world of EFTS, where transactions will be conducted over the wire, these statutes may fall by the wayside. The banking statutes currently provide for up to five years in prison and/or up to $5000 in fines for anyone who embezzles funds from a federally insured financial institution.[13] These statutes, though, only cover employees, officers, and agents of these institutions; outsiders are not covered. Under an EFTS, the statutes would be of little value where outsiders with access to the system (i.e., a store clerk) could transfer funds to their accounts or those of associates. Further, these bank statutes provide for the unlawful taking of "funds," "money," or "securities." Under an EFTS, funds, money, and securities will differ from their present meanings. Paper will be substituted by electronic impulses. Could these be defined as being *funds* within the present statute? At least one court has held no.

Title III of the Omnibus Crime Control and Safe Streets Act makes it a federal offense for anyone to willfully intercept any wire or oral communication.[14] This act may have some application where bugging is involved. However, if the intercepted messages are coded (as they probably will be in an EFTS), then the act may be of little use to the prosecutors. The fact that the messages may be coded should be no obstacle to felons, though, for they have demonstrated an ability to obtain access to such codes. Further, an entire black market in computer access codes or codes as they relate to the transmission of messages could easily spring up.

The Federal Consumer Credit Protection Act makes it a federal offense to use fictitious, forged, or fraudulently obtained credit cards.[15] The act is intended to prevent felons from obtaining goods or services through such credit cards. Under EFTS, if identification cards were employed only to effect deposits or withdrawals of funds, the act would be of no value to prosecutors. If, however, such cards were employed to obtain services or goods, the act might come into play. However, there would be no jurisdiction under this act in noncredit transactions.

The Fair Credit Reporting Act was passed by Congress in 1970, with the objective of protecting the consumer from unreasonable invasions of his privacy by credit companies.[16] The act applies to information collected by banks, credit card companies, and other credit-reporting agencies. These institutions are required to keep current records. Upon request, they must provide the consumer with all the information contained therein, and the sources of such information. Civil remedies are available to the consumer, and there are provisions for criminal sanctions against firms or individuals who obtain information about consumers under false pretenses. To date, however, the criminal sanctions have never been fully employed. Consumers are limited, because of limited finances, in bringing civil action to enforce the act. Admittedly, the statute has fallen short of its objectives. Whether it would be of value under EFTS remains to be seen. The federal agency charged with ensuring compliance with this act is the Federal Trade Commission. This agency, unfortunately, has shown a lack of prosecutorial vigor and commitment in the past. It is doubtful that it will fare any better under a more demanding EFTS environment unless its present investigatory and prosecutorial structure is altered.

Modern criminals have shown an uncanny ability to adapt to a changing environment. While computer technology has already given rise to new forms of crime, EFTS will provide additional fertile ground for the sophisticated and well-organized criminal elements of our society. It may also foster a greater internationalization of crime. Groups on several continents could conceivably work together to coordinate their attacks on EFTS. Our present investigatory and prosecutorial apparatus has been too slow and cumbersome to meet the challenge of the white-collar criminal. The latter, armed with the technology of EFTS, could indeed pose a formidable challenge. Whether we can meet this challenge will depend greatly on our ability to change and adapt to the demands of white-collar crime. Time will tell.

Notes

1. Jerry Knight, "Giant Food Accelerates Computerization Plans," *Washington Post*, September 21, 1977, pp. E-1, E-2.
2. "Sears To Experiment with Plan for Electronic Share Drafts," *Washington Post*, September 16, 1977, p. D-13.
3. "Global Banks Transfers To Become Swifter," *Washington Post*, September 23, 1977, p. D-13.
4. August Bequai, "A Survey of Fraud and Privacy Obstacles to the Development of an Electronic Funds Transfer System," *Catholic University Law Review* XXV (Summer 1976):771.
5. "Electronic Banking Aims at Business," *Business Week*, January 24, 1977, p. 77; see also, "Those Buck Passing Machines," *Money Magazine*, February 1976, p. 46.
6. Bradley Graham, "Banking Revolution Is Still Underway," *Washington Post*, June 25, 1977, p. D-8; see also, Stuart M. Speiser, "Abolish Paper Money and Eliminate Most Crime," *American Bar Association Journal* (January 1975):47.
7. See August Bequai, *Computer Crime* (Lexington, Mass.: Lexington Books, D.C. Heath, 1978), for a review of the problem of futuristic computer crimes.
8. Phillip J. Scaletta, "Privacy Rights and Electronic Funds Transfer Systems—An Overview," *Catholic University Law Review* XXV (Summer 1976):801.
9. August Bequai, "The Cashless Society: An Analysis of the Threat of Crime and Invasions of Privacy," *Journal of Contemporary Law* III (Winter 1976):47.
10. Jules Bernard, "Some Antitrust Issues Raised by Large Electronic Funds Transfer Systems," *Catholic University Law Review* XXV (Summer 1976):749.

11. See 31 U.S.C., secs. 1082, 1101(a), and 1121(a); the act's constitutionality was upheld by the U.S. Supreme Court in *California Bankers Association* v. *Schultz*, 416 U.S. 30 (1974).

12. 18 U.S.C., secs. 1341 and 1342.

13. 18 U.S.C., secs. 656 and 657.

14. 18 U.S.C., secs. 2510-2520.

15. 15 U.S.C., 1644.

16. 15 U.S.C., 1681.

Conclusion

In 1205 one of the longest suits in recorded history began in India; it was finally settled in the mid-1960s. Another long suit began in mid-nineteenth century France and ended more than 100 years later. If foreign cases hold the record for longevity, American litigation is certainly by far the most voluminous and costly in the world. For example, one California case produced more than 20,000 pages in transcripts and more than 500 exhibits. It took more than 17 weeks to select a jury, and the trial itself cost over $2 million. One present federal suit involves more than 100 million pages of documents, thousands of witnesses, and more than 3000 exhibits. The cost has run into the millions of dollars, with no end yet in sight.

The cost of litigation in this country exceeds the annual gross national product of many small nations. Litigation of every kind has become extremely expensive. The prosecution of one antiwar figure ran over $3 million. White-collar crimes have proven, more than other forms of litigation, to be extremely costly and time consuming. Voluminous pages of documents, numerous witnesses, and armies of attorneys are usually involved. At present, few prosecutorial offices have the funds and manpower to handle these costly and time-consuming cases. A complex fraud case could easily bankrupt a local prosecutorial office. Unless the cost of litigation is brought down, white-collar felons may thwart the law by simply making it too costly to prosecute them.

Our sentencing model also leaves much to be desired. For example, a 22-year-old alien who had illegally entered the country received three years of imprisonment from a court; a 25-year-old involved in a bank robbery received 10 years of imprisonment. A study of some 300 white-collar felons showed that those involved in frauds averaging over $22 million received prison terms of one year or less; those involved in frauds averaging $21 million received suspended sentences, fines, or probation. By comparison, in Israel a felon involved in a $1 million fraud received 15 years of imprisonment.

Our entire penal model was designed to deal with traditional criminals, those of the lower classes who were involved in common-law crimes. For example, in deciding on whether to place an individual on probation, a judge looks at such things as the offender's emotional maturity; use of drugs, alcohol, or other dangerous substances; his family status and stability; and the neighborhood from which he comes or intends to live in. The judge also considers such things as the offender's employment plans. When applying this criteria to a convicted white-collar felon, it becomes meaningless; it is not a true yardstick of whether he continues to pose a threat to society. A more realistic yardstick is needed; the penal model itself needs to be reviewed.

171

If we are to curb white-collar crime, it is not enough to simply modernize the investigatory and prosecutorial machineries. We need to also look at the judiciary and at the many laws that we presently have on our books. Many of these are antiquated and create environments in which frauds flourish. For example, many cities have numerous ordinances that regulate the construction industry. In some cities it is impossible for a construction firm to abide by these regulations; consequently, public officials are bribed. Many of our social programs, both federal and local, have no built-in safeguards; as a result, they easily fall prey to swindlers.

Equally important, the climate in this country for too long has been one of "get away with what you can." That era has come to an end; our limited air, water, and land resources no longer make this possible. The energy crisis has not only given rise to new frauds but also to an impetus to imprison these swindlers. Our precarious international standing, and the global balance of power, has given rise to investigations concerning national defense contracts.

The growing concern with white-collar crime is an outgrowth not only of an educational process that found impetus in the consumer revolution of the last 15 years but also of a realization that this country's resources are no longer unlimited. There is no new frontier left to tap. We must preserve and use wisely what we presently have. This growing class of criminals, armed with the tools of modern technology, threatens this very delicate equilibrium. They threaten our very social, economic, political, and environmental fabric. Lest we curb them, they may bring our downfall. No modern society can long tolerate a $40 billion annual rip-off.

Bibliography

Allen, Brandt R. "Embezzler's Guide to the Computer." *Harvard Business Review* 53 (July 1975):79-89.

_____ . "Computer Fraud." *Financial Executive* 39 (May 1971):38-43.

Aubert, Vilhelm. "White Collar Crime and Social Structure." *American Journal of Sociology* 58 (November 1952):263-271.

Balter, Henry G. "Plea Bargaining and the Tax Fraud Syndrome." *Tax Magazine* 52 (June 1975):333-339.

Barmash, Isadore, ed. *Great Business Disasters: Swindlers, Bunglers, and Frauds in American Industry.* Chicago: Playboy Press, 1972.

Baruch, Hurd. *Wall Street Security Risk.* Washington, D.C.: Acropolis Books, 1971.

Becker, Joseph M. *The Problem of Abuse in Unemployment Benefits.* New York: Columbia Univ. Press, 1953.

Benson, George C.S., and Thomas S. Engerman. *Amoral America.* Stanford, Calif.: Hoover Institution Press, 1975.

Bequai, August. *Computer Crime.* Lexington, Mass.: D.C. Heath, 1977.

_____ . "Litigation under the EFTS." *Federal Bar News* 23 (June 1976):174-177.

_____ . "Crooks and Computers." *Trial Magazine* 12 (August 1976):48-53.

_____ . "Wanted: The White Collar Ring." *Student Lawyer* 5 (May 1977):44-48.

_____ . "The Binary Burglars." *Student Lawyer* 5 (February 1977):18-24.

_____ . "White Collar Plea Bargaining." *Trial Magazine* 13 (July 1977):38-43.

_____ . "Legal Problems in Prosecuting Computer Crimes." *Security Management* 21 (July 1977):26-27.

_____ . "White Collar Muggers Have Reason to Feel Safe." *Barrister* 4 (Summer 1977):26-29.

_____ . "The Forty Billion Dollar Caper." *Police Chief* XLIV (September 1977):66-68.

_____ . "Computer Fraud: An Analysis for Law Enforcement." *Police Chief* XLIII (September 1976):54-57.

_____ . "The Cashless Society: An Analysis of the Threat of Crime and the Invasion of Privacy." *University of Utah Journal of Contemporary Law* 3 (Winter 1976):46-60.

_____ . "The Electronic Criminal." *Barrister* 4 (Winter 1977):8-12.

_____ . "The Impact of EFTS on Our Criminal Justice System." *Federal Bar Journal* 35 (Summer 1976):190-205.

_____ . "Prosecutorial Decision-Making." *Police Law Quarterly* 4 (October 1974):34-42.

———— . "White Collar Crimes—The Losing War." *Case & Comment* 82 (September 1977):3-10.

Black, Hillel. *The Watchdogs of Wall Street.* New York: William Morrow, 1962.

Blum, Richard H. *Deceivers and Deceived.* Springfield, Ill.: Charles C. Thomas, 1972.

Bowley, G.F. "Law Enforcement's Role in Consumer Protection—Consumer Protection Symposium." *Santa Clara Lawyer* 14 (Spring 1974):447-450.

Brodsky, Edward. "Self-Incrimination in White Collar Fraud Investigations: A Practical Approach for Lawyers," *Criminal Law Review* 12 (March-April 1976): 125-139.

Butler, Robert N. "Why Are Older Consumers So Susceptible?" *Geriatrics* (December 1968): 83-88.

Caldwell, Robert G. "A Re-Examination of the Concept of White Collar Crime." *Federal Probation* 22 (March 1958): 30-36.

Caplin, Mortimer. "The IRS, Racketeers and White Collar Criminals." *American Bar Association Journal* 62 (July 1976): 865-866.

Caplovitz, David. *The Poor Pay More—Consumer Practice of Low Income Families.* New York: Free Press, 1963.

Carey, Mary, and George Sherman. *A Compendium of Bunk or How To Spot a Con Artist—A Handbook for Investigators, Bankers and Other Custodians of the Public Trust*, Springfield, Ill.: Charles C. Thomas, 1976.

Carke, Thurstan, and John J. Tigue, Jr. *Dirty Money—Swiss Banks, The Mafia, Money Laundering and White Collar Crime.* New York: Simon & Schuster, 1975.

Carmier, Frank. *Wall Street's Shody Side.* Washington, D.C.: Public Affairs Press, 1962.

Carper, Jean. *Not with a Gun.* New York: Grossman, 1973.

Clinard, Marshall B. *The Black Market—A Study of White Collar Crime.* Montclair, N.J.: Patterson Smith, 1972.

Dershowitz, Alan M. "Increasing Community Control Over Corporate Crime—A Problem in the Law of Sanctions," *Yale Law Journal* 71 (September 1961): 289-306.

Dietrich, Noah, and Robert Thomas. *Howard: The Amazing Mr. Hughes.* Greenwich, Conn.: Fawcett, 1972.

Dirks, Raymond L., and Leonard Gross. *The Great Wall Street Scandal.* New York: McGraw-Hill, 1974.

Domhoff, G. William. *Who Rules America.* Englewood Cliffs, N.J.: Prentice-Hall, 1967.

Ducovny, Amram M. *The Billion Dollar Swindle—Frauds against the Elderly.* New York: Fleet Press, 1969.

Edelhertz, Herbert. *The Nature, Impact, and Prosecution of White Collar Crime.* Washington, D.C.: Government Printing Office, 1970.

Edgerton, Henry W. "Corporate Criminal Responsibility." *Yale Law Journal* 36 (April 1927):827-844.

Emerson, Thomas I. "Review of White Collar Crime by Edwin H. Sutherland." *Yale Law Journal* 59 (January 1950):581-585.

Erdman, Paul. *The Silver Bears.* New York: Simon & Schuster, 1974.

Farr, Robert. *The Electronic Criminals.* New York: McGraw-Hill, 1975.

Fellmeth, Robert C. *The Interstate Commerce Commission.* New York: Grossman, 1970.

Fuller, John G. *The Gentlemen Conspirators: The Story of Price-Fixers in the Electrical Industry.* New York: Grove Press, 1962.

Gardiner, John A. *The Politics of Corruption: Organized Crime in an American City.* New York: Sage, 1970.

Geis, Gilbert. *The White Collar Criminal.* New York: Atherton Press, 1968.

Gentry, Curt. *The Vulnerable Americans.* Garden City, New York: Doubleday, 1966.

Gibney, Frank. *The Operators.* New York: Harper, 1960.

Griblin, August. "Beware—Computerniks at Work." *The National Observer*, May 23, 1977, pp. 1, 15.

Grimes, John A. "Equity Funding: Fraud by Computer." *American Federationist* 80 (December 1973):7-9.

Hadlick, Paul E. *Criminal Prosecutions under the Sherman Antitrust Act*, Washington, D.C.: Ramsdell, 1939.

Hay, George A., and Daniel Kelley. "An Empirical Survey of Price-Fixing Conspiracies." *Journal of Law & Economics* 17 (April 1974):13-29.

Hills, Stuart L. *Crime, Power and Morality—The Criminal Law Process in the United States.* San Francisco: Chandler, 1971.

"Hot on the Scent of Payoffs at Home." *Business Week*, March 8, 1977, pp. 29-30.

Hutchison, Robert A. *Vesco.* New York: Praeger, 1974.

Jenkins, Jon A. "Working for Uncle Sam: The Flyaway Problem of Federal Attorneys." *Student Lawyer* 5 (April 1977):48-54.

Katona, George. *Price Control and Business.* Bloomington, Indiana: Principia Press, 1945.

Kefauver, Estes. *In a Few Hands—Monopoly Power in America.* Baltimore: Penguin, 1965.

Kohn, E.J. *Fraud.* New York: Harper & Row, 1973.

Kwitney, Jonathan. *The Fountain Pen Conspiracy.* New York: Knopf, 1973.

Leff, Arthur A. *Swindling and Selling.* New York: Free Press, 1976.

Leigh, Leonard H. *The Criminal Liability of Corporations in English Law.* London: Weidenfeld & Nicolson, 1969.

Lipson, Milton. *On Guard: The Business of Private Security*. New York: Times, 1975.

Maxa, Rudy. *Dare To Be Great*. New York: Morrow, 1977.

McKnight, Gerald. *Computer Crime*. New York: Walker, 1973.

Nader, Ralph, and Mark Green. "Crime in the Suites." *The New Republic*, April 29, 1972, pp. 17-21.

Nash, J. Robert. *Hustlers and Con Men—Anecdotal History of the Confidence Man and His Games*. New York: Lippincott, 1976.

Parker, Donn B. *Crime by Computer*. New York: Scribner, 1976.

Paulson, Morton C. *The Great Land Hustle*. Chicago: Regnery, 1972.

Randal, Donald, and Arthur P. Glickman. *The Great American Auto Repair Robbery*. New York: Charterhouse, 1972.

Robinson, Kenneth. *The Great American Mail Fraud Trial: USA v. Glenn Turner and F. Lee Bailey*. Plainview, New York: Nash, 1976.

Steele, Eric H. "The Dilemma of Consumer Fraud—Prosecute or Mediate." *American Bar Association Journal* 61 (October 1975):1230-1234.

Stern, Philip M. *The Great Treasury Raid*. New York: Random House, 1964.

Sutherland, Edwin H. *White Collar Crime*. New York: Holt, Rinehart, & Winston, 1949.

Whiteside, Thomas. "Annals of Crime (Computers—II)." *New Yorker Magazine*, August 29, 1977, pp. 34-64.

Williams, Roger M. *The Super Crooks*. Chicago: Playboy Press, 1973.

"Your Finances Bared (But Who's Looking)." *Money Magazine* 6 (May 1977):85-88.

Index

About the Author

August Bequai is a practicing attorney in Washington, D.C., specializing in legal aspects of technology. A former federal prosecutor and chairman of the Federal Bar Association's Subcommittee on White Collar Crime, he also has been vice-chairman of the Federal Bar Committee on Criminal Law and presently chairs the Subcommittee on Computer Legislation for the American Society for Industrial Security.

Bequai holds the J.D. from The American University Law School and the L.L.M. from the National Law Center of the George Washington University. He is an adjunct professor of criminal law at The American University and has lectured widely before numerous law-enforcement and business groups such as the FBI Academy, The Institute on Organized Crime, The American Society for Industrial Security, The National Association of County Attorneys, and many others. Mr. Bequai has authored more than thirty articles dealing with various aspects of the law as well as a contributor to the *Maryland Jury Instructions in Criminal Cases.* His *Computer Crime* was published in 1978 and he is currently working on a book on organized crime.